# DEMOCRACY DENIED

D0869084

# DEMOCRACY DENIED

## DESMOND WILSON

MERCIER PRESS

MERCIER PRESS
PO Box 5, 5 French Church Street, Cork *and*
16 Hume Street, Dublin 2

*Trade enquiries to CMD DISTRIBUTION,*
*55a Spruce Avenue, Stillorgan Industrial Park, Blackrock, Dublin*

Published in the US and Canada by the
IRISH AMERICAN BOOK COMPANY
6309 Monarch Park Place, Niwot, Colorado, 80503
Tel: (303) 625 2710, (800) 452-7115
Fax: (303) 625 2869, (800) 401-9705

ISBN 1 85635 177 7

10  9  8  7  6  5  4  3  2  1

*A CIP record for this book is available from the British Library.*

*Printed in Ireland by Colour Books Ltd.*

# CONTENTS

# 1
# THE SETTING

To be born in Belfast may seem a misfortune, to stay living and working there a mistake. But that is not how it is.

The six county government directly and through its agents created one major uprising against its Catholic population for every 12 years of the state's existence. Belfast was the scene of some of its worst excesses. The organisation of pogroms was an old and well tried tactic, such uprisings having been engineered for decades even before the six county state was invented. One of the reasons the six county state was founded was that anti-Catholic government did not work exactly as planned – it was meant to ensure that all Ireland would stay under British control. When this proved impossible and a new six county state was cut away from the rest of Ireland, government policy in London and Belfast was to ensure that this new state at least would always remain under British control. The policy was pursued recklessly and ruthlessly.

Belfast suffered as a result not of people's misfortune but of repressive government policy to which a majority of its citizens gave their consent.

On the other hand it was near Belfast and with the help of Belfast merchants that the Society of United Irishmen was founded, bringing into Ireland the ideas of freedom, equality and respect which were expressed in the rhetoric of the American and French revolutions. McCracken, Orr, Neilson, Hope and a host of others inspired Belfast with ideas of freedom and found inspiration in it.

Some Belfast merchants profited from the slave trade. Some profited from the atrocious working and living conditions of the workers who filled their mills and workshops:

> There weren't any health or safety regulations. Most of the women who worked in the mill had very bad feet, because they stood in water all the time. They had leg ailments because of the time they

had to spend standing. And they had very bad chests because of the pouce that was in the air. There were people who had 'pouce chests' because their complaint came from the stuff that came off the flax.[1]

On the other hand, some Belfast merchants and others, like Thomas McCabe and Mary Ann McCracken said 'No' to the slave trade. 'May God waste the hand of any who would embark on such a nefarious enterprise; may he be condemned to eternal hell', thundered McCabe.[2] Some employers tried to improve the living conditions of the workers within the narrow limits imposed upon them by their commercial world which was ruthlessly ambitious and greedy. Workers were easy to please; some of them, like Mrs Wynne, remembered in their old age that Quaker proprietors gave them porridge in blue rimmed bowls at eight in the morning after two hours work in the linen mills and by this simple act earned the reputation of being good employers:

> We would go to Mass at a quarter to six on holy days of obligation. If we were late coming into work we had to go through the office and we would be fined and lose a penny out of our wages. A thing about Greeves, they were said to be Quakers and they were very good people. You could get porridge, you could order it, at half eight. The price was taken out of your wages, a penny for the porridge and a ha'penny for the milk. You couldn't afford it every day. I still remember the lovely white bowl with the blue rim round it, it was gorgeous ...[3]

On the edge of the Belfast swamp the grim task of survival made people recognise that even the least sign of benevolence was helpful.

Belfast like all other places has its contradictions. Living and working there one becomes part of the contradictions, respecting the place because its people are your own while trying with desperation and often anger to change what you cannot tolerate of its cruelties.

When I was ten my father brought me to see the street barriers put up to separate Catholics from Protestants in the

Dock area in 1935. Like so many others I was led to believe that Catholics and Protestants could not live together in peace. It was many years before we admitted to ourselves how untrue that belief was. We could live together in peace as well as any people in the world as long as we were allowed to. The devices preachers and politicians used to make sure we would not be allowed to were similar to those used by agitators elsewhere, but in Belfast they seemed able to survive longer. A mere four years before the year 2000 Paisley, a Christian preacher, howling about the whore of Babylon and Christian men beating police with pikes on the Ormeau Bridge were considered normal by citizens whose intolerance was encouraged by their leaders' political foolishness and by a religious depravity long abandoned in the rest of Europe.

We accepted the myth that we could not live together in peace partly because we knew no better and partly because we were afraid to contradict the mythmakers. We took a long time to realise that when comfortable – and often well-educated – people said it they were offering us one of the greatest insults you can hurl at any people – that we lacked the basic human quality of being able to live with other human beings. The myth was expressed so often that we seldom thought of questioning or contradicting it. If we had done so we would have been accused of being mad or subversive – mad to question those who taught us the myth and subversive for revealing the real reasons why good people in Belfast were so successfully persuaded to fight each other.

The people of Belfast, and of the six counties as a whole, are normal. But thousands of halls, lodges, associations, interest groups, clerical and political factions not only kept enmity alive among them but even resurrected it when citizens by the normality of their lives had allowed it to die. Most of us accepted the government version of ourselves, that some higher authority had to teach us manners and while they were doing so we had to be kept apart; that the manners were to be taught by churches and church schools and keeping us apart was a matter for police and if necessary soldiers.

Some of us never got rid of the idea that we were incapable of living together in peace, but others seeing how degrading, untrue and cynical it was rejected it, only to understand how little we could do to get rid of it. Some of those who professed to teach us manners made life intolerable often and unshareable always, while those paid to keep us apart did so with a proficiency that included assassination and torture.

Academic, clerical and rich theoreticians preached and perpetuated the myth, the enforcers did what they were handsomely paid to do to reinforce it.

Clerics and academics were among our most effective agitators, although they always accused poor people with little education of being responsible for the riots which followed their speeches. No riot or public upheaval happened without clergy in the background urging people against each other now, condemning them afterwards. Without such academic and clerical agitators the six counties would have been spared much of the suffering it had to endure.

If ever there was any danger of citizens generously sharing their dreams, their work, their genius and their vision of the future they could create together there was always a Professor Savory of Queen's University, or a Councillor Longbottom of Liverpool or Cooke, or Hanna or Drew to stir them up against each other again and convince them it was impossible because God did not want it.

Organised violence was not planned, incited and paid for by poor citizens but by the rich and educated. Professor Savory had an excuse for the bitterness of his speeches about Catholics. He came to Ireland from the Channel Islands, a descendant of Huguenots who fled from a cruel regime run by French Catholics. But for all his education he did not appreciate that the Catholics of Belfast in his day were not same people who revoked the 1598 Edict of Nantes or the persecutors of his people or anyone else's.

Churchmen said that if you drew a map and marked on it all the places in the six counties where violence occurred these would coincide with areas of deprivation and unemployment. Their conclusion was, as always, that poor people were to blame for the ills that hurt them more than others. But if you drew a map and marked on it all the places where violence was planned and paid for, these would coincide with the areas where the rich and well educated lived and prospered. Patrick Shea, one of the few Catholics to reach a high position in the six county regime's civil service admitted that this was so:

> There have been occasions when, under the stress of material deprivation, they (poor people) looked like making common cause and turning their combined anger on the people or the institutions whom they saw as their oppressors, but any such moves were brief and unproductive. A prudently-dropped hint from a more affluent area, a suggestion that 'the others' at the end of the street were plotting to take over, a whisper of 'Popery', invariably put up the shutters against collaboration.[4]

The gun-running through Larne in 1914 was financed, as was the Ulster Unionist Party, by rich business people and landowners. Fred Crawford, a British army Lt Colonel, who arranged the importation for the UVF shows in his book *Guns for Ulster* how he and the other gun-runners were in constant contact with people in important positions in business and English politics to get money and other support, in spite of the fact that the UVF intended to use the guns to fight not primarily the nationalists but the British government.[5] Another member of the British armed forces, Lt Colonel Sir Wilfred Spender, wrote the foreword to Crawford's book, praising the enterprise, telling how Spender revived the UVF in 1920 at the request of Carson and Craig. Spender, who had been involved in the gun-running became head of the six county civil service, responsible for shaping the regime.

Academics as agitators, military officers as gun-runners, clergymen as preachers of hate, the wages of their sin was the death of citizens who were too poor to be able to make major decisions about their own lives and too powerless to enforce the minor ones they were allowed to make.

If local agitators were not enough, or if the citizens seemed to be drifting together again against the best interests of the ruling gentry and the factory owners, others were brought in from outside, preachers from Liverpool or Glasgow, ex-priests from Spain, to light up any embers of religious conflict that remained to be blown upon. The *Ulster Protestant*, journal of the Ulster Protestant League, was an early instrument of bitter propaganda, Paisley's *Protestant Telegraph* another among many. Rallies in the Ulster Hall and country marquees, often under the guise of religious revivals renewed the fervour of those whose rage against their Catholic fellow citizens was flagging in spite of the persistent and normal urging of preachers and politicians.

## THREAT WAS EVERYWHERE

When a group of Christian citizens set up an organisation called Platform in the hopeful 1960s they held their first public conference on the topic of fear. They believed that if fear were removed from our society, the agitators and power groups would be faced up to for the first time and, being bullies, would collapse. Thirty years later pervasive fear was still an issue, but by then even the anti-Catholic agitators and preachers were feeling afraid and were loud in their protests about it. Fear was now serving the wrong masters.

The inexorable movement towards change which began with the Civil Rights movement in the 1960s 'hardened a conviction in the bulk of Protestants that the union with Britain was indeed being undermined, and in larger and larger numbers they turned for reassurance to Ian Paisley, the very man whose self-fulfilling prophecies had started the whole process'.[6]

Paisley, like all successful preachers attracted the crowds because he made them afraid of demons which only he could exorcise. The demons, they found to their astonishment, were their Catholic neighbours.

When a major anti-Catholic uprising was imminent, the Belfast air became thick with fear as the religious secret societies prepared their annual festivals and the city, always threatening, became abnormally so.

With discipline strict in workplace, home and school, with preachers making one set of people afraid of another now, and all of them afraid of damnation hereafter, with an ever present danger on its streets Belfast was a grim place to live in and children grew into adults with fear all around and even inside them. None of them could grow up without experiencing one, two or more of the recurring pogroms. Fear was so pervasive that people stopped noticing they had it and seldom even began to ask the reasons why.

Those brought up in this culture of fear were surprised to see a new generation of young people growing up who did not have it. The optimism of these young ones, their lack of fear, their dignity and their indignation made older people realise, many of them for the first time, how brow-beaten they had been and how cultivated terror had darkened their lives. The parents of the 1920s had to survive, the next generation had to survive and then lift up their heads. Successive generations had to assess respectfully the limitations and achievements of their fathers and mothers and build yet another platform from which even more progress could be made towards a decent society.

For those of us determined that the older ones should survive with optimism, the younger ones with dignity and all of us with indignation, the most pressing task was to dissolve the fear for good, so that Belfast's new citizens could create a better life than any of us had had so far.

That is what the six county conflict from the 1960s to the 1990s was about.

# 2

# THE IMPERIAL BARGAIN

The six county state was born in 1921 because the British imperial government needed to keep power in Ireland with as little expense of soldiers and money as possible. They used the same methods to achieve this as in other parts of the world where they had a problem of the same kind.

When the First World War ended in 1918 armed conflict did not end. Rival imperial governments still wrangled and if necessary fought to keep territories they already had or to win new ones. But the people of France and Britain were tired of destructive wars and becoming more conscious of how their money should be spent. The costs of the war in human lives and money had been atrocious. They wanted an end to the waste of both. Troops must be brought home and money spent at home to provide what had been promised, lands fit for people who had made such sacrifices. British troops demanded to be sent home. Five thousand of them rebelled at Calais. Churchill wanted them back home as soon as possible.

Most people in Britain had not been aware of how much they had lost. Although during the war whole streets had been devastated as news poured in of the dead and wounded from monstrous futile battles, only the government knew what the total losses were and how much money it spent for purposes the public knew nothing about. It spent eleven million pounds to subsidise one revolt by Emir Hussein against the Ottoman Empire; it had half a million men on Turkish soil and suffered hundreds of thousands of casualties.[1]

The loss of human life in Europe at this period was appalling – eight and a half million had been killed by the war, 20 million by the influenza epidemic. Britain needed over a million troops at one time to keep its hold in the Middle East, but by making new political arrangements reduced this number dramatically to just over three hundred thousand by 1919.

Lloyd George said it required six million pounds a year to hold Palestine. *The London Times* said British people were spending a hundred million a year in the Middle East and commented unfavourably on the 150 million spent abroad. In July 1921 Britain's spending abroad was so unbalanced that *The Times* editorial declared, 'While they have spent nearly 150 million pounds since the Armistice on semi-nomads in Mesopotamia they can find only 200,000 pounds a year for the regeneration of our slums and have had to forbid all expenditure under the Education Act of 1918'.[2]

Two sets of interests then had to be satisfied: the demands of people to have their families reunited with a higher standard of living and the need of imperial governments to hold on to overseas possessions with as little expense of troops and money as possible. There were many areas in the world where Britain was, or wanted to be, dominant and its interests had to be protected. The Middle East was one of them. Ireland was another.

The historic reasons for Britain's occupation of Ireland were Britain's defence needs and to ensure British control of the Irish economy. Britain needed a safe western flank, cheap food, plenty of workers and army recruits and no competitors. These needs were seen as crucial until 1990 when the British government through its secretary of state for the six counties Peter Brooke said it no longer had any selfish strategic or economic interest in remaining in Ireland. This was an authoritative statement that the historic reasons for Britain's occupation of Ireland no longer existed. In the 1920s, however, they did.

In the Middle East at the end of the First World War Britain no longer had the resources to hold all the territory over which it had had military control during and immediately after the war. It was disputing control of territory with the French, it feared intrusion into it by the Russians. So it receded into small corners and drew new boundaries, making political arrangements which would ensure that British interests would be protected for the foreseeable future. New states were created, Kuwait being one of them, new boundaries were drawn.

It was an era in which Middle Eastern countries and frontiers were fabricated in Europe. Iraq and what we now call Jordan, for example, were British inventions, lines drawn on an empty map by British politicians after the First World War; while the boundaries of Saudi Arabia, Kuwait and Iraq were established by a British civil servant in 1922 ...[3]

Within such new boundaries the British imperial government set up or encouraged the setting up of regimes which were unchangeable by democratic process, and which would maintain British interests in the area. It also kept control of strategically useful ports outside the newly created boundaries – for example the ports from which they controlled what remained of the old Turkish empire. The new boundaries cut across existing ethnic, cultural and religious lines and still cause unrest, division and war in the Middle East. In other areas similar arrangements were made – Yugoslavia and Czechoslovakia also were artificial entities created after the First World War.

The Arabic-speaking section of the Ottoman Empire had now been politically redesigned ... in the east Kurdish, Sunni, Shi'ite and Jewish populations had been combined into a new Mesopotamian country named Iraq, under the rule of an Arabian prince; it looked like an independent country, but Britain regarded it as a British protectorate. Syria and a greatly enlarged Lebanon were ruled by France. A new Arab entity that was to become Jordan had been carved out of Palestine; and west of the Jordan river was a Palestine that was to contain a Jewish National Home ... Churchill had achieved the principal objectives he had set for himself in the Middle East ... His over-riding goal had been to cut costs and he had done so drastically. Moreover he believed that he had created a system which could be operated economically in the future. His line of air bases stretching from Egypt to Iraq allowed him to keep the Middle Eastern countries under control with a minimum of expense.[4]

Troops could be sent home, money was saved and British interests were secure for decades to come. This process in the Middle East was being created between 1919 and 1921. At much the same time a similar process was in hand in Ireland.

Winston Churchill and Lloyd George were among the same British politicians involved in both.

In Ireland revolutionary forces were defeated in 1916 but the defeat was temporary. The revolution began again in 1919 and ended with Britain making new imperial arrangements in 1920–21 for safeguarding its interests in Ireland. It drew a new border which cut across already existing ethnic, cultural and religious lines. In a newly created state in the north-east it set up a regime which was unchangeable by democratic process and would uphold Britain's interests in Ireland. It kept control of strategic ports in that part of Ireland which had become independent. The newly drawn border ran through formerly integrated territory, through villages and even houses; it ran through Anglican and Roman Catholic dioceses, Presbyteries, Methodist circuits.[5] 'At its inception the boundary bisected 1,400 farm holdings, villages and even private houses. It cross-cut several water systems and 20 railway lines of which only one remains today'.[6]

In the newly created state in Ireland's north-east there was an implied promise, as there was in the newly created regimes in the Middle East, that if the regime was threatened, from inside or outside, imperial troops would be available to defend it. In the six counties British troops were used during the next seventy years to quell disturbances within the state, for example during the anti-Catholic pogroms of the 1920s and the anti-government demonstrations of 1932. In 1969 the most serious deployment of troops in support of the regime took place when the six county state was in danger of destabilisation.

Most of the time during the first five decades of the six county state's existence however the troops kept a discreet distance from the people. The full scale deployment in 1969 became necessary when the police in the six counties were unable to control a threatening situation which seemed to the government to be developing into a revolution. By this time, 1969, the troops were no longer seen as 'imperial', except by a few. The empire which so many boundaries had been redrawn to preserve was now dissolved. The arrangements made – in vain –

to keep it intact were, however, still causing bloodshed in Ireland and elsewhere.

The creation of the six county state then was to protect not Irish Catholics or Protestants but the interests of an imperial government using the same methods as it did in other parts of the world. If we abandon the model of Britain redrawing boundaries in Ireland in order to protect the interests of Irish Protestants and use instead the model of an imperial government securing its own interests with minimum expenditure of troops and money we understand more clearly what happened then and since.

Many in Ireland refuse to accept any model for the six counties other than that of Protestant/Catholic or nationalist/unionist antagonism with the British government standing between two factions uneasily keeping the peace:

> Northern Ireland, then, was not created to satisfy any local demand for self-government. No one in Ireland of any political persuasion wanted or welcomed it. Its creation was an expedient imposed on the country by a hard-pressed British cabinet, which sought only to hold two groups of Irishmen from each other's throats and to give them an opportunity of living peaceably apart, since they could not live peaceably together.[7]

The conclusion from this analysis is that democratic government is impossible until the citizens are taught to live together in peace and until then Britain must remain in control. Continuance of British rule then is the logical conclusion.

But since British imperial interests dictated the creation of the six counties and its democratically unchangeable government, a more logical and democratic conclusion is to say that this imperial arrangement which the British government no longer needs and the Irish people never wanted should now be dissolved. Robert McCartney who favours total integration of Ireland's north-east with Britain remarked, 'Westminster legislated for devolution only in the one region of the United Kingdom where not only was it not wanted, but it would do incalculable harm'.[8] Given the imperial needs and methods of the time it could not be expected to do anything else, no matter what ethnic, religious and social upheaval might result. The dissolution of the imperial arrangement when it is increasingly wasteful and harmful would serve the best interests of both Britain and Ireland.

The Protestant/Catholic analysis of the six counties seems reasonable if we do not investigate real causes. Any other analysis frightens journalists whose newspaper, radio and television companies would reject it. Conflict about the pope, about marches, about identities and inter-community tension is said to be the primary cause of the political problems of the six counties but this is a secondary conflict which could die of its own accord if not artificially kept alive by those who have an interest in it. Most people are too occupied with day to day survival to question the Protestant/Catholic analysis offered to them and this is one reason why it survives. The analysis of the six counties situation which says Protestant/Catholic antagonism is the primary problem may stem from internal racism, that is, racism directed not against another people but unwittingly against one's own:

> Scientists may think they have discovered primitive life on Mars, but the truth is anyone watching events in Derry this weekend, Drumcree a month ago, and Anglo-Irish relations for the past 800 years would be convinced that *homo sapiens* – and particularly the Irish variety – is the most primitive organism in the universe (*Sunday Tribune*, 11 August 1996).

Once the British imperial government had secured its interests in Ireland by installing an unchangeable pro-British regime in the north-east and a regime in the south which could not or would not threaten its interests, the strategic ports it held in the independent part of Ireland were no longer necessary and it withdrew from them in 1938. Britain further reduced its troop commitment in Ireland by giving the six county government power and money to set up a local police and militia while imperial troops were on stand-by and would have to be housed somewhere anyway. It had also reduced costs by demanding an imperial contribution from the six county area it occupied and land annuities from the part of Ireland which it had left.

For the Irish in the six counties and the south this meant a significant loss of resources but for the British government it was not only a cost cutting exercise but one in which the six county Irish would pay something for their own occupation and those in the south a great deal for their freedom.

The six county government was given the most lucrative tax area in Ireland but was allowed to keep only a small proportion of the taxes and made to pay the imperial contribution. Eventually the six county government was relieved of payment of the imperial contribution because it could not afford it and by 1964 the British government was subsidising the six counties by 81 million, 165 million in 1965, by 481 million in 1987 and by 1,760 million a year in 1983. In return for this massive subsidy which grew more and more as the years passed to become four billion in 1995 the British government had what amounted to a massive military base which was available also to NATO or any other military body of which Britain might become a member.[9] If kept within bounds some expenditure was worth the money, especially as the United States was also an interested party during the anti-Russia phase of western policy. In the south the payment of annuities to the British government was stopped under the leadership of Eamon de Valera, although the British government of that time still demanded and got a substantial lump sum by way of final payment.

Britain had its military base in Ireland, a measure of control of the Irish economy and money and troops had been saved.

The British government did not move to create democratic government in the north-east, whether demands were made for it in the Belfast parliament, in street demonstrations or through armed revolution. Secure tenure and stability had to be obtained and political thinking at the time dictated that the most effective way to achieve these ends was to set up new states and hand over control to governments which could not be changed by democratic means and would be protected from internal or external threat by imperial troops. A senior British official acknowledged that in the six counties this is what was done.[10] The results of the 1918 election were used, he said in

1974, to ensure 'a Protestant majority big enough to be certain that democratic principles, self-determination, the wishes of the majority, plebiscites, elections, would infallibly produce the same results forever'.

The 1920 Government of Ireland Act by which the imperial arrangement was made assumed, on paper, that Ireland would be reunited and indeed made provision for this:

> With a view to the eventual establishment of a parliament for the whole of Ireland and to bringing about harmonious action between the parliaments and governments of Southern Ireland and Northern Ireland ... there shall be constituted a Council of Ireland ... On the date of Irish union the Council of Ireland shall cease to exist and there shall be transferred to the Parliament and Government of Ireland all powers then exercised by the Council of Ireland ...[11]

Irish nationalists therefore found the imperial redrawing of boundaries if not acceptable, less unacceptable because it seemed it could only be temporary. But British policy was to make sure that it would be permanent in spite of its own law. The government said publicly that the six north-eastern counties could opt out of an independent Ireland for one year, but told Edward Carson, a unionist leader, privately that whether these counties willed it or not they were to be kept out of a United Ireland for ever.[12]

In 1945 a British cabinet accepted that in no circumstances could the six counties cease to be part of the United Kingdom. In 1949 the policy as expressed by Norman Brooke cabinet secretary to the British prime minister was the same.[13] The territory was needed for strategic reasons. This determination of the British to keep the six counties was shown also in a Commonwealth Relations Office study released in 1982: 'Failing some firm and satisfactory assurance as to the attitude in war of a united Ireland ... there are strong strategic arguments for the retention of the friendly bastion of the Six Counties'.[14]

Foreign Office papers of 1952, Royal Air Force Marshall Slessor, Michael Mates and Farrar-Hockley at various times have made this determination clear. In the 1970s William Whitelaw, secretary of state, said that in the six counties the unity of the United Kingdom was an issue. John Major indicated the same in the 1990s. The six counties, it had been decided, were to be ruled in the British interest for ever. In the 1920s it had to be for military and economic reasons. In the 1990s these reasons were gone, but new reasons took their place. Most important among them was that if the six counties were lost the United Kingdom might begin to disintegrate.

# 3
# Myths and Mythmakers

The six county state had a government which could not be changed by democratic means, subsidies from the British government and a guarantee of imperial military intervention if this should be required. It needed all this to survive. It also needed survival myths and a language in which to express them.

Myths and language exaggerated what was important to the six county regime and minimised everything else. Constant use of the name 'Ulster' gave the impression that the territory the Unionist Party controlled from 1921 onwards was bigger than it really was. In the 1920s the Irish province of Ulster consisted of nine counties with a population of 1.6 million, the new state comprised only six of these counties with a population of 1.270 million. The historic Ulster had a Catholic population of 700 thousand (about 43%) and 900 thousand Protestants. In the new state which excluded three of the nine counties Catholics were only 34.8% in 1924. The Unionist Party had a larger majority of Protestants than in the traditional province of Ulster, which seemed to ensure that the regime could never be changed in the foreseeable future by democratic means unless a significant number of Protestants changed their allegiance. A change of allegiance was made unlikely by constant propaganda from politicians, press and pulpit and because of the penalties for dissent, loss of job, reputation, social standing or life.

The myth that the regime controlled the whole traditional Ulster province was expressed and strengthened by newspapers. The *Belfast Telegraph, Belfast Newsletter* and *The Northern Whig* constantly referred to 'Ulster' even when the events reported referred only to the six counties. Constant repetition of the name impressed it on the minds of readers until it became accepted by most of them. In the *Belfast Telegraph* of 30 August 1996 the term 'Ulster' occurs 26 times, but always in relation to matters concerning the six, not the nine, counties. In the same edition of the newspaper the term 'Northern Ireland' is used 22 times and the term 'province' three times. In each case the term denotes a territory larger than that actually controlled by the Stormont or Westminster governments. Sometimes the result had been bizarre as newspapers and orators referred to some aspect of the economy of Ulster but were not discussing that of Donegal, Cavan and Monaghan, almost as if these counties no longer existed. Language which inflated the size of the state was still considered necessary even 75 years after its foundation.

The name Ulster was attached also to the Royal Ulster Constabulary, the Ulster Defence Regiment, the New University of Ulster, Ulsterbus, Ulster Television, BBC Radio Ulster and other organisations although none of these had any official function in the three Ulster counties outside the six county state.

Cardinal Conway when opposing the campaign of the IRA said, 'a million Protestants in N. Ireland can not be bombed into a United Ireland'. A million Protestants who could be bombed into anything did not exist in the state, as the census figures showed. In 1921 there were 820 thousand Protestants in the six counties, forty years later there were nearly 876 thousand. Always less than 900,000 the Protestants were assumed to be in favour of the British union; most were, some were not, but people came to believe there were a million Protestants in the north-eastern state all of whom were unionists. There were not.

In 1994 when it appeared that Catholics were now 43% of the total population of the six counties, this percentage shocked those who had always believed the myth of the million. Catholics had made up 43% of the total population of the original province of Ulster, so three counties were rejected from the new six county state to reduce their proportion in the state to about a third, but by the 1990s Catholics had become 43% of the population of the truncated province as well. The problem confronting the British was similar now to that of 1921. Could they keep permanent control if Catholics became a majority and continued to oppose the British union? A number of choices were open to them.

Either they could repartition the six county state, carving out another area whose government the inhabitants could not change by democratic means and which would resemble Gibraltar. Or they could apply the same procedures of population control as in the past including enforced emigration, population control and pogrom. Or they could try to make the union attractive for Catholics by fair employment and opening up to them the possibility of taking part in government. In the 1919–21 period they chose partition, one party unchangeable government and population control. As the year 2000 drew nearer these methods were more difficult to use and the British government's needs had changed. Such forcible and expensive occupation of the whole six county area or repartition might not serve Britain's interests.

A favoured solution was to convince the unionists that they should concede limited democratic government with structures specially designed to suit local conditions. One party in government, the rest in opposition was not practical for democratic government of the six counties and was probably by now unsuitable for government anywhere. Whether London kept overall control or not, it seemed that the north-east would have some autonomy, so power sharing within it was a reasonable device for governing. A problem for the British however was that sharing government would probably in time lead to a fusion of interests between Catholic and Protestant middle classes who would then look for freedom from London not because they were being persecuted but because they believed they would become more prosperous without London hanging round their commercial, industrial and social necks. New forms of government which were necessary for Britain to keep control of the six counties now would almost certainly lead to its having to leave in the foreseeable future.

The rise of the Catholic population to 43% made it urgent for the British government and its Irish supporters to decide whether they should continue the policy of reducing the Catholic population by forced emigration, pogrom and ghettoisation or try through normal politics to create a regime in which the state could be stabilised by the consent and co-operation of some of the Catholics, who might one day become a majority. The confrontation between the Orange Order and the British government at Drumcree in July 1996 showed starkly how bitterly and deeply the two opinions were held by each faction among the unionists. The clergy-led order insisted on marching through a Catholic area on their way from a Church of Ireland service and organised widespread disruption and intimidation to force the British government to allow them to do it. Michael McGoldrick, a Catholic, was murdered. As in 1914, unionists were threatening not only their Catholic fellow citizens but the British government. The British government might envisage limited relief for Catholics in order to keep control of the state, the Orange Order would not.

Using the word 'million' to describe under 900,000 was not a great mathematical fault. But it had a greater emotional effect than 'nine hundred thousand' and gave a political message. Maximising what belonged to the regime and minimising the rest helped to create the myth that Catholics were 'the minority' when in reality they were the largest religious group in the six counties, in Ireland as a whole and in the European Community . The 'majority' in the six counties was created by a political union of smaller religious groups, principally Church of Ireland, Methodist and Presbyterian, each of which was smaller in number than the Catholics and all of which were very different from each other in teaching, belief and practice but united in opposition to Catholic political and economic power. If the Catholics ceased to be seen as a threat the divisions among this politically cohesive but religiously fragmented majority would probably have appeared starkly.

Many Catholics accepted the title 'minority' imposed on them. They thought it was better to avoid religious labels, and that this might better underline the disabilities they suffered – in many countries there was greater awareness of suffering 'minorities' than of suffering 'Catholics' or 'Jews' or other specific groups. But Catholics sometimes internalised the label imposed on them. Monsignor Murray an American, having visited

Ireland said in a submission to the Catholic hierarchy of the United States that for the sake of peace they should refer to Catholics not as Catholics but as 'the Minority' when speaking about the six counties. The bishops took his advice because it seemed to strengthen their case when speaking to those who were sensitive to the rights of minorities in America, but the psychological cost of accepting the label was high for Catholics in the six counties. There had to be a special feeling of power-lessness among people who although belonging to the largest religious group in Ireland, the six counties and the south, the largest practising group in Britain, the largest religious group in the European community had consented humbly to call themselves 'the Minority'.

Towering above this self deprecating minority there proud-ly stood the Ulsterman who according to the myth was gifted with straight speaking, honest dealing and a special work ethic.

The Ulsterman whether understood as belonging to the six or the nine county division was not particularly efficient, hon-est, neat or straight-talking, although the myth was success-fully fostered that he was – women were not regarded as im-portant in the myths of the state although tens of thousands of women signed their own version of the Ulster Covenant in 1912 vowing to oppose Home Rule in Ireland. For those who be-longed to the Orange Orders or Freemasons there were many things they could not talk about or do whether straightly or otherwise. Many Protestant Ulstermen in the six counties be-longed to the Orange Orders or the Freemasons or both. Many in the other three, Donegal, Monaghan and Cavan, belonged to them as well – the Orange demonstration at Rossnowlagh, Co. Donegal, in July 1996 attracted 7,000 people, representing a large proportion of the Protestant male population of the Re-public pledging allegiance to the British monarch.[1]

The influence of the secretive Orange Order was both to promote members and to silence them. 'It counted prior to the 1970s among its membership virtually all unionist members of parliament whether at Stormont or Westminster and in con-sequence all members of the Stormont government. Membership was an indispensable condition of political advancement'.[2]

For a citizen who did not belong to them their machinations were damaging, and their everyday secrecy irritating. In a barber's shop the conversation might open like this: Hello Sam, how's things? Response: do you know your neighbour? The signal between barber and customer indicated that the man in the barber's chair was not one of them. Orange and Masonic secrecy silenced the straight-talking Ulsterman even in the most banal circumstances. Conversation in a pub would be inhibited when a customer sitting at the bar passed his whiskey glass under his chin in a gesture to fellow masons that a brother in the craft was there.

Jesus Christ said that what was whispered in rooms would be shouted from house tops; the Masonic and Orange Ulstermen whispered in rooms what could well have been shouted from rooftops. Or in the pubs. Or at the barber's.

Such control of what ordinary Ulstermen could say and do could only be imposed by an association which counted among its members men in important positions in the church and state. Since its foundation in 1795 the Grand Orange Lodge of Ireland counted among its Grand Masters four earls, one duke, one army general, two colonels, two army captains, a number of members of the British parliament and one clergyman. Many Presbyterian and Church of Ireland clergy belong to the Orange Order or the freemasons or both. There are Orange and Masonic lodges for politicians, journalists, local councillors and other specialised groups. The late Bishop R. C. Elliott, who was a member of both organisations was the last Archbishop of Armagh to show his membership of the Orange Order publicly by marching in their processions. One of the few attempts by aspiring politicians to break the Orange Order's hold on political offices was that of Basil McIvor who won a parliamentary seat without being a member of the religious order.[3]

During most of the lifetime of the Stormont regime it was advisable for people looking for promotion to be members of the Orange Order. Both the Unionist Party and the administration were dominated in turn by the Orange Order. In 1924 Sir Robert Lynd said that the RUC was identified with the Orange

Order, that is, it was not, as is often assumed, simply a Protestant force, it was dominated by one section of the Protestant population. Monsignor Denis Faul wrote:

> The British army has never been used to clear away Orange road blocks. This is an example of state control by secret societies such as the Orange Order and Freemasons. There are 2,000 Orangemen in the RUC and several hundred masons ... The RUC with its ranks peopled by Orangemen faces the Orangemen.[4]

Clergymen, police and politicians are among those whom a community expects to be plain-speaking and honest rather than inhibited by the rules of secret societies. In the six counties the myth of the plain-speaking Ulsterman was built up against a background of organised secrecy and fear which affected every walk of life and made it impossible to speak one's mind without carefully weighing up the political, religious and economic consequences of doing so.

From time to time the power of the secret orders to restrict what people could say emerged among clergy. Bishop Butler preaching at the funeral of Lord Craigavon said that if as prime minister he had behaved in a more enlightened way the six counties might have been a happier state; for this he was publicly abused.

Rev. Armstrong was dismissed from his Presbyterian church in Limavady for having fostered good relations with neighbouring Roman Catholic clergy and had to go to Oxford where he then worked as an Anglican.

John Armstrong, Anglican Archbishop of Armagh, was filmed with Cardinal Ó Fiaich commenting upon a crisis in the prisons. He said that some aspects of the treatment of prisoners should be examined by the government. He received phone calls into the early hours of the following morning and retracted his statement. The callers included local members of the Masonic and Orange Orders.

Alan Whicker and Ed Murrow, internationally known journalists, were silenced by the BBC under pressure from the the six counties unionists; John Hewitt the poet who had to leave the six counties to work in Coventry and Sam Thompson, author of the play *Over the Bridge* were among the writers for whom plain-speaking meant considerable financial and other loss. The press as James Kelly points out after a lifetime as a journalist in the six counties, 'treats the establishment there with kid gloves'.[5]

Some of the liberal clergy defended the Orange Order and the state in spite of their record of imposed secrecy and intimidation. The Rev. James Haire, on the liberal wing of Irish Presbyterianism, told the United States Presbyterians in 1972 when the six counties were experiencing some of the most severe problems of intimidation, displacement and sectarianism, that in the six counties there was full religious freedom, and defended the Orange Order as a force for good like the trades unions. Haire had significant experience of discussing the six counties problems with Catholic clergy and others and had been made aware of the grounds on which their charges of religious abuse were based. But at this time liberal Presbyterian clergy were trying to influence their church to be open to change and were afraid to acknowledge such abuses lest they alienate members of the church who said they did not exist or if they did exist were being effectively dealt with. A blunt plain speaking Ulsterman was not only rare but courageous.

Inefficiency, considered a deplorable lapse elsewhere, was built into the six counties' system. Terence O'Neill, once prime minister, in his autobiography tells part of the story with remarkable frankness. He had never been opposed in an election from 1946 until Paisley challenged him in 1969. The system was so constructed that for most of the lifetime of the state it was not worth while to try to unseat about half the unionist members of parliament. Craigavon while prime minister could spend a whole winter in Australia and New Zealand and no one would comment on it. It was a part time government (described by a journalist as a government of threes, three hours a day, three days a week, three months in the year) in which a minister could still survive by attending one day a week; at whose insistence motorways were built not because there were vehicles to fill them but because as part of the United Kingdom 'Ulster' should have them.

Catholics who were one-third of the population in the 1920s and 43% by the 1980s, were excluded from most posts of responsibility and even from many minor posts from which they could have advanced towards it. Gallahers, the biggest tobacco factory in the world, in the 1980s employed only a small number of Catholics.[6] Their intelligence and skills could not be used in government, big business or social development. Women were unlikely to be given positions of influence or control. They were poorly represented among unionist politicians.

The north-east then was run by the brains, industriousness and business acumen of, at best, one-third of the population. The idea that a small area like the six counties needed the brains and enterprise of everyone in order to survive, let alone prosper, was put forward enthusiastically in the optimistic 1960s, but rejected at that time by those who had the power to make the necessary changes.

The pool of intelligence and initiative was reduced even further. Teachers were forbidden to be members of local councils. Of all Protestants eligible for appointment or promotion, it was the members of the secret Orange and Masonic societies who had the best chance of significant advancement. The pool of available talent was thus reduced to a degree which inevitably resulted in inefficiency. The exclusion of Catholics reduced the pool by one-third rising to 43%, the exclusion of most women reduced the remainder by almost half, while the preference for members of the secret societies reduced the available pool of ability even further. Yet another selective process favoured Trinity College, Dublin, graduates in the six counties civil service. Thus the vast majority of people in the six counties were excluded from playing a significant part in its development. No state could continue to exist with such built in constrictions.

Professor Richard Rose of Edinburgh University adverted to this in his studies of the six counties situation in the 1970s but did not seriously question the viability of a state which excluded so many of its citizens from decision-making. Like most commentators he was concerned with community relations rather than efficiency of government.[7] For him as for many others the efficiency of the six county state was taken for granted.

More homely evidence of the built-in inefficiency of the six county state was given by bus drivers who complained that they watched helplessly while secret society members who could not adequately read and write were promoted to positions which required both, while they, who could read and write, were passed over. This was true in the 1940s and remained true in the 1990s.

The shipyards suffered also. Robert Johnstone paints a disheartening picture:

> In the main yard workers had to bribe the crane drivers to lift their materials; the crane drivers were so poorly paid that they demanded 'blood money' before they would lift things. This was supportable by large gangs of men, but single workmen could not afford to pay and so had to struggle up the ladders carrying whatever equipment and materials they needed. No doubt the casualty figures of men falling off the staging were not helped by such practices ...
>
> The system could mean that the men had the freedom to feel that they were sometimes beating the system. The 'homer', the object made in work for use or sale at home, was a legendary phenomenon; many brass pokers must stand even today at firesides in front rooms across the city. Tins of battleship grey paint decorated homes during the Second World War. At one time Queen's Island men were said to form the bulk of the audience at cinema matinee performances. And during the slump of the thirties when there was no work those who could not be sacked might find a quiet corner for sunbathing or borrow a boat and row across to the entertainments of York Street.[8]
>
> Belfast shipyard was badly damaged and of low productivity during World War Two.[9]

Another writer is critical of wasteful standards which had to be accepted in the Belfast shipyards in the 1970s:

> It was difficult to explain in public that the main problem for government at the time was not how to expand employment in Harland and Wolff but how to improve productivity by getting about two-thirds of those who were there out of it without

actually causing a riot.[10]

> Harland and Wolff where the workers existed on the state's bounty to the extent that they did not even recover the cost of materials, making the shipyard the biggest occupational therapy workshop in Western Europe.[11]

A record like this might be discovered in an industrial enterprise anywhere but in the six counties there was a politically constructed myth that government supporters were exceptionally efficient, honest and possessors of an extraordinary work ethic. The myth of the work ethic was based upon a number of assumptions but also upon a command by St Paul in his second Letter to the Thessalonians: 'While we were with you we used to say to you, "Whoever refuses to work is not allowed to eat". We say this because we hear that there are some people among you who live lazy lives and who do nothing except meddle in other people's business. In the name of the Lord Jesus Christ we command these people and warn them to lead orderly lives and work to earn their own living'.[12] In the course of the industrial revolution this was taken not as a command to work hard for the sake of the community but rather as a justification for starving the unemployed.

People who suffer from such exclusion often find other opportunities to prosper. Some of the Catholics and Presbyterians forbidden professional positions under the penal laws after the battle of the Boyne, made a living and prospered through business. The tourist industry in the six counties is founded on the work of men who came to Belfast looking for work, taking the few jobs available in public houses, and developing their liquor businesses into lounges and hotels and eventually into the sophisticated hotel industry which is the basis of the six counties tourist trade. The liquor trade was for historical reasons run largely by Catholics, hence the present involvement of Catholics in the hotel industry which contributes substantially to the six counties' economy. While in the early days of the state Protestant leaders and business people professed to despise the trade, as time went on it became more prosperous and significant. Licensing laws which had always been restrictive against public houses, largely owned by Catholics, and permissive towards clubs many of which were under Protestant majority membership, changed. Ownership of public houses changed through normal sale and also during pogroms, as Rev. Carson points out in his book, *Church, State and Industry*. Carson was Church of Ireland rector of the enormous parish of St Patrick in East Belfast. Off-license premises were a primary target of arsonists during the pogroms because they were owned by Catholics and had been subject of persistent anti-alcohol preaching. When the Catholic owners had to flee, their premises were taken over by some of Carson's parishioners and soon re-opened under Protestant management. In the pogrom of 1969 onwards over 600 public houses were attacked or destroyed and many of the lucrative premises changed hands at prices favourable to the new owners. As the pattern of ownership changed laws and attitudes to drink changed. Anti-alcohol preaching became less strident, enforcement of laws less harsh.

During the 25 years war it was the clubs – now popular in areas which people were afraid to leave for downtown amusements – that became the target of harsh laws, while public houses were relatively favoured by the authorities.

Inefficiency became part of the six county system. The shipyards were expensively subsidised and for many a hive of idleness, proud to have built a ship which was the biggest in the world but sank on its first voyage out due to 'bad luck, human stupidity, laziness and disorganisation'.[13] Belfast merchants and politicians erected the *Titanic* memorial now standing in the grounds of Belfast's City Hall which commemorates 'the courageous men' lost on the ship but makes no mention of the women or children. Exclusiveness included even the dead.

The British government in subsidising the shipyards and other enterprises subsidised not only industry but also inefficiency. In exchange it was content with an enormous military base from which it could never be dislodged. When Harold Wilson examined the books in 1974 and made his greatly resented remark referring to people in the six counties as 'spongers' this is what he had in mind, an economy in which people did not have to be efficient because subsidies from other people's taxes shielded them from the consequences of their inefficiency.

During the 25 years of war (1969–1994) money was poured into the state but little development resulted. Projects rejected elsewhere were brought hastily into undeveloped areas with sometimes disastrous results. De Lorean in the early 1980s cost more than 80 million pounds for jobs which did not last. Church based organisations and others involved not in business or industry but social management, received millions of pounds for job promotion projects:

> The Catholic Church in West Belfast has been transformed into a business empire which currently controls 500 jobs, representing an annual contribution from government funding of approximately 3 million pounds. The business will shortly benefit from the inflow of approximately 100 million over five years, which has been earmarked by government for industrial development in West Belfast.[14]

The number of new jobs created by these projects was small, most of the jobs unproductive. People in hitherto impoverished and neglected areas were also learning now that inefficiency was encouraged and promoted at great cost within the system.

One of the myths on which the state was founded and which helped it to survive is that of the incompatibility of Catholics and Protestants. Their inability to live together in peace has been accepted as the reason for what is called 'The Troubles'. The use of this term, 'The Troubles' is itself a means of perpetuating a myth. Over twenty-five years of what would be described elsewhere as a revolutionary war were described not as such but rather as 'troubles'. The term suggests that ungovernable people are restless, that they have to be kept in order by rulers who sometimes may be obliged to keep them apart and sometimes may encourage them to come together but only under the benign leadership of a government which in either case allows them no real power to govern themselves. Using the term 'troubles' to describe the conflict in the six counties effectively hid what was really happening to the people.

The reality was that there was a series of attacks on the Catholic population designed to keep the voting pattern constant, in areas where an upset could have serious consequences for the union and the government. In the 1920s the Stormont government abolished proportional representation because it posed a threat to its majority. In the following decades the voting pattern was kept constant by constructing electoral boundaries favourable to the government and by forceable relocation of sections of the population. Major anti-Catholic uprisings occurred, on average, once every 12 years for this electoral purpose. These were officially represented as popular uprisings of Protestants against Catholics. It was often said however by people who suffered in them that the uprisings and evictions were engineered 'from outside' the districts in which they occurred. Although this might seem an excuse to shift the blame from the neighbours of evicted Catholics, it seems to have been true. The uprisings and evictions were not popular uprisings by bigoted Protestants against their Catholic neighbours but a carefully orchestrated re-arranging of the voting pattern which was done as often as was needed.

From the 1920s the ruling party, with British government subsidies, created a patchwork of industrialised and non-industrialised areas in the six counties. Some areas had substantial industry while others within a short distance of them had not. The areas designated for substantial industrial development were those in which the vote for the union with Britain was high, while areas where the pro-union vote was low were under-developed. East Belfast was favoured as against West Belfast, within West Belfast Shankill was favoured as against the mainly Catholic Falls district. Derry was under-developed, Antrim and Ballymena well-developed. Where industries existed near or within areas with a significant Catholic population Protestant workers were if necessary bussed in, sometimes under armed guard. Tiger's Bay was favoured as against New Lodge. Areas east of the River Bann were favoured as against those in the west which had a significantly larger Catholic population. It was assumed that Catholics and areas where Catholics were in the majority were against the union and government policy was to restrict Catholic economic and voting power.

Catholics migrated to find work. They might go to Britain, America or Australia, and thus leave a voting area. But they might instead go just a few miles away to a pro-union and largely Protestant area. They were allowed to do this as long as work was available – although they would not hope to get the best of the jobs – and as long as their increasing numbers did not upset the voting pattern in any district.

If the voting pattern did change, safe unionist areas could become less safe, marginal areas could be lost. When this danger arose from an increasing number of Catholics going to work and live in any area a major pogrom against them was created. Preachers gave inflammatory sermons, politicians accused the Catholics of being subversive and both warned against the encroachment of Rome into the lives of Ulster Protestants.

In July and other times when political feeling ran high such public agitation was particularly effective, reinforcing the unpublicised propaganda going on continually in the secret lodges and some of the small Christian chapels and halls. This process of agitation and eviction in the East Belfast of the 1920s is described by Rev. Carson. The Orange Order was an instrument used to foment the agitation.[15]

The result of uprisings of this kind was that Catholics fled into safe areas, for example, parts of West Belfast. In the East Belfast Catholic school of St Columcille's the number of pupils was reduced from 700 to 100 by the major pogrom of 1969 and the succeeding years. A North Belfast Catholic parish suffered a similar loss of population. The scale of the evictions can be appreciated from this and from figures given in official and other reports.[16]

The Falls Road area of West Belfast has layer upon layer of refugee families and their descendants with a history of flight from such attacks from the 1920s and 1930s to the massive flight in 1969 which was described as the biggest forced movement of population since the Second World War.

# 4
# ATTACK AND DEFENCE

In August 1969 when Catholics in Belfast were attacked in one more major anti-Catholic uprising between 8,000 and 10,000 people fled their homes, most of them into the Catholic areas of West Belfast. The city's welfare arrangements broke down. The civil service and other agencies must have foreseen that this disaster was coming but their welfare and other services failed almost at once. This was probably due not only to inefficiency but to their expectation that the pogrom would be fast, furious and decisive.

As the situation developed and local people provided care for refugees the public services moved quickly not only to provide for the homeless but to recover control of whatever was being or should be done for them. Many years later they had recovered control to a large extent but never completely.

Mothers and children were in special need. Local people received the refugees into their already overcrowded homes and the schools which they had opened with or without the permission of school governors.

## THE IRISH AND BRITISH RED CROSS ARRIVED

A pre-occupation of the British Red Cross was to make sure the Irish Red Cross and the volunteers working with the refugees were aware that only the British Red Cross was entitled to operate in this area. The Irish Red Cross was entitled under its own rules to operate only in areas governed from Dublin. This had to be made clear. Another pre-occupation was that all money donated for relief, whatever its source, should be channelled through the British Red Cross. Yet another was to stop people using the red cross emblem on vehicles carrying refugees and furniture into West Belfast from areas under attack. Volunteer drivers in cars and lorries feared for their safety as they passed through areas where they might be attacked. They painted a red cross on white sheets and put them on their vehicles. The British Red Cross protested vigorously and demanded that they be removed because only they had the right to use such a flag. They did not however offer to provide safe conduct for refugees in vehicles of their own.

Apart from such pre-occupations the Red Cross did little. Most of the relief work for refugees was done by local people who used the few resources they had while the Red Cross, churches and other agencies looked after what they saw as their own interests and tried to make sure especially that all monies coming in for relief were in their hands.

This Belfast experience of the Red Cross was not unusual. A religious sister who worked in Biafra thought it not worth while to discuss what the Red Cross had done during the war there. In Norway a social worker pointed out that there was a difference between a local Red Cross organisation anywhere in Europe and the International Red Cross. The International Red Cross did important work efficiently for prisoners and refugees; local Red Cross associations raised money to cope with disasters which they did not normally have to deal with themselves. At a local level they were not equipped to deal with anything but the smallest emergency. Those who never had to deal with severe communal distress ran garden parties to raise money for those who did. The people in West Belfast soon learned that while they did the work, the organised welfare and other bodies would insist upon holding the money and the power.

> In a way this incident (flying the red cross flag) exemplified the dual standards of the fur-coated charitable sector in Belfast at the time, which found it easier to cope with an earthquake in Nepal or floods in Bangladesh, or to respond to famine in the Horn of Africa, than to deal with the refugees or casualties of indigenous beastliness in Belfast. I have never subscribed to the Red Cross since.[1]

From 1969 onwards the public authorities were to be engaged in a long struggle to win back powers and functions they had let slip away from them. People would create alternative arrangements for education, leisure, cultural development, would set up alternative political parties, alternative media of communication, even alternative policing and an alternative army. Approaching the last years of the century the public authorities had succeeded in winning back some of these functions which they regarded as their own, settling for limited control of others, trying to re-establish the police and facing the almost impossible task of dismantling the alternative armies.

Meanwhile the unwillingness of public authorities to allow citizens to take over their own defence was to be proved in a dramatic way.

Catholics had few guns to defend churches and homes as they came under attack. Republicans who had been militarily active in the past were among the few who knew where the guns were and how to use them. In 1968–69 clergy asked them to protect the churches and gave them meals and a few comforts while they did it. Between 1969 and 1972 twenty-one Catholic churches were attacked as well as schools and parochial houses. One of the republicans, Billy McKee, was seriously injured defending St Mathew's Catholic church in East Belfast.

Other republicans protected Clonard Monastery in West Belfast. Once the police had been reinforced by the military, however, and the church authorities believed their buildings were safe they dispensed with the services of the republicans and others who had defended them. The republicans were once again looked upon as opponents.

Since the police often led the loyalist crowds attacking the Catholics it became clear once again that if Catholics were to be protected now or in the future, there would have to be fundamental changes in how the state was run or they would have to protect themselves. Making significant changes in the state would take many years, protection was needed now.

Meetings were held in halls, sometimes parochial halls with the consent of clergy, and the people demanded weapons for protection. The only place they were likely to get them was Dublin. Some people went there to ask for them. The Dublin government was content to allow things to get worse in the six counties in the hope that the British would have to intervene decisively to lance the boil of consistent misrule there but some members of the governing party, Fianna Fáil, were not content with this. They understood, as the Catholics in the six counties did, that the unionist government could not or would not reform itself, it had to be reformed from outside and the only agency for doing this was the London government, without whose subsidies the regime could not continue.

Most southern politicians, backed by the newspapers, would have settled for firm and lasting British control of the north-east, provided the British made promises to treat Catholics fairly, even if there were no firm guarantees that they would keep their promises. Most Catholics in the six counties, always hoping that the state was reformable and its leaders open to reasonable argument, were prepared to settle for fair government within the state as it then was. Republicans believed that such hopes were vain and made preparations accordingly.

At first the Dublin government showed signs of being willing to help the Catholics in the six counties in the way they wanted to be helped. Promises were made that arms would be made available, a few men were trained in the use of weapons in Dunree, a quiet camp in Co. Donegal.[2] Irish army rifles were moved up to Dundalk.

It soon became clear however that Jack Lynch's government in Dublin had no intention of giving guns to Catholics in the six counties. If they had they could have done so within days. The guns brought to Dundalk were put under lock and key and a Dublin government minister, Gibbons, admitted later in court that the operation was a public relations exercise. Catholics were being reassured without being helped, unless just reassuring them was help.[3] Apart from such reassurance the government in Dublin meant to take no effective action. The training camps in Donegal were also a reassurance exercise, training men to use guns they were never going to get.

The British government had responded to citizens' demands for Civil Rights by attacking those who asked, and the Dublin government backed by churches and news media now demanded that Catholics should rely for protection on the

British government which, they professed to believe, would eventually persuade its supporters in the six counties to stop attacking them.

In Belfast Catholic Church officials moved to take control of the Citizens Defence Committees which had been set up in many areas to defend the residents from attack. The church authorities in Belfast directed clergy to take control of these committees and bring them all under one organisation, the Central Citizens Defence Committee whose chairman would be appointed by the local bishop. At a meeting to arrange this takeover of control by clergy one priest dissented, asking, What happens if we find that some Citizens Defence Committees are asking for and getting guns? Are clergy prepared for the consequences? It is for people other than clergy to decide whether there should be guns or not.

The answer from the church authorities was firm: If you do not do it somebody else will.

But the church authorities had no intention of putting clergy in the position of asking for or getting guns. Their intention was to prevent the Citizens Defence Committees from getting any. The Dublin government and church officials were afraid of power coming into the hands of republicans or even of the people in general. Catholic Church leaders agreed that Civil Rights should be granted in the six counties but these should be achieved by interaction between the Dublin and London governments, and between Catholic Church officials and the Stormont and London governments. Any intervention by others which tended to upset this balance of negotiation was resented. Catholics had to be protected but this protection was to be obtained through negotiation with police, military and government. If the Citizens Defence Committees were allowed to continue they could gain control of a political process which should be controlled primarily by governments and churchmen and secondarily by politicians approved by them. Some Defence Committees were asking for guns for protection from Dublin and the church's intention, and that of the government in Dublin, was to take control of the committees as part of their strategy to make sure the guns did not come.

Church policy was to convince people they should rely upon government for protection rather than learn to protect themselves. The taking down of street barricades at the urging of Bishop Philbin and other churchmen was evidence of this policy. It did not take long for the Citizens Defence Committees to be brought under church control, given new premises and equipment and reduced to an agency for issuing statements. Republicans and others meanwhile went their own way and succeeded in getting guns whether church or governments willed it or not. Catholic Church policy had ensured that the church would become less and less effective in persuading the British or in curbing the republicans.

The fear which Dublin government and church officials had of republicans and socialists made it urgent however that on the one hand the London government should be seen to respond to demands from them, that the Catholics should be protected and on the other that republicans and socialists should be quelled. Neither Catholic Church authorities nor Dublin government approved of putting guns into the hands of republicans, socialists or the people involved with neither who flocked to the parochial halls demanding protection. Jack Lynch in another context had warned people against the socialism of the largely middle class and conservative Irish Labour Party; Bishop William Philbin had warned Catholics, in relation to the largely middle class and conservative Civil Rights movement, not to be 'led by the reds'. Both might well have added, 'Better dead than defended by republicans or socialists'.

The strategy of the church and the Dublin government was to satisfy republicans and others with promises sufficient to persuade them not to take matters into their own hands, while at the same time trying to persuade the British to grant Civil Rights against their own will and that of their loyalist supporters. The British government itself found a commitment to Civil Rights in the six counties politically impossible. If they created the radical changes necessary for democratic government in the six counties this could create a constitutional crisis in Britain itself. The advanced form of democracy such as would be required to create equality in the six counties would be demand-

43

ed in other parts of the United Kingdom. Church leaders and Dublin government officials, however, professed to believe they could persuade the British government to bring about fundamental democratic changes against the wishes of its supporters in Ireland and its own interests at home.

As soon the British government made a promise to protect the Catholics, the republicans and others who had protected the churches were dismissed and came under severe attack from all the churches for the next 25 years.

The people who went to Dublin for guns for protection were promised they would get them.[4] The movement of guns to the border and the opening of training camps gave the impression that the promise was sincere. The promises however were gestures. The training camps and the movement of guns were gestures.

Ordering guns from Continental Europe was also a gesture. An order was given from Dublin to Germany, for rifles and ammunition to be sent to Ireland. These weapons were to be put into safe-keeping so that if the attacks in the six counties became very severe again the people would have weapons to defend themselves. The arms were ordered but never arrived in Ireland. Instead, those involved in getting them and two cabinet ministers who had been designated to help the people under attack in the six counties were arrested. The reason given by the government in Dublin for the arrest and eventual trial of one of its own ministers who was not involved in the arms deal, one of its own army officers who was, a six county civilian and a Belgian businessman was that the order for arms was not authorised by the government and had to be stopped. The accused, Mr Haughey, Captain Kelly, Mr John Kelly and Mr Albert Luycx were acquitted. The trial failed to establish satisfactorily, one way or the other, to what extent the attempted importation was officially sanctioned.

If the government in Dublin had seriously intended to supply arms to those under attack in the six counties they could have done it from their own supplies. Precautions would have to be taken, as Captain Kelly pointed out, but this would be simple. Doing this, however, could have brought the matter to the attention of Irish army officers, many of whom would not approve of such help being given to six county Catholics. If the Irish police got to hear of it, the plan was finished. Some of them, as was revealed in Richard Deacon's biography of Maurice Oldfield, once head of British intelligence in Ireland, were working for British intelligence, so any gun-importing plan could have been undermined through the activities of those who were and the scruples of those who were not.

The arms ordered for the protection of Irish Catholics did not arrive in Ireland. Word of the order reached the Special Branch. Their senior officers and members of the parliamentary opposition put pressure on the Lynch government. So did the British government. The people most easily blamed were arrested and brought to trial.

After the IRA ceasefire in 1994 when the British government made 'decommissioning' of IRA weapons a precondition for Sinn Féin to be admitted to talks, this bizarre and sordid series of events was remembered. If Catholics were attacked again who would defend them? The RUC led the major anti-Catholic pogroms in 1969 and were actively anti-Catholic before and since; British military from England, Scotland and Wales were being taken off the streets and it was unlikely that the British government would agree to be so heavily involved militarily again; locally recruited British military, the UDR, later renamed the Royal Irish Regiment, could not in any circumstances be accepted as a force to protect Catholics; the Dublin government had shown that it was prepared to make gestures, but it also arrested and put on trial those who had organised defence for their fellow citizens in the six counties. Confidence in the United Nations as an effective protective agency had been eroded by its international failures of the past decade. In the six counties its presence might be not only futile but damaging.

Since no protecting agency could be identified it was logical for people to believe that if the IRA gave up its arms a hundred thousand unprotected Catholics might well have to flee over the border under attack from those who realised that the Catholics now once again formed almost exactly the same proportion of the state's population as they did in 1921. The treatment such refugees would get when they arrived would probably be similar to that given by the government to the refugees in 1969–70. No one who knew what happened in that period relished the thought of allowing it to happen again, however hospitable individual citizens and informal groups had been.

The only reasonable alternative to depending for defence on a hostile government or on a presumably friendly government promising guns which never arrived and transporting guns from one locked armoury to another with instructions not to distribute them, and training men how to use guns they would never get, was self defence. The IRA might one day again have to be part of that defence and meanwhile the arms in their dumps would be a useful deterrent. Even Fr Denis Faul, a strong opponent of republicans, admitted that for Catholics to have access to weapons for defence was a prudent policy, not an act of aggression.

For the six county Catholics the keeping of such guns was a matter of prudence rather than a threat that they would be used. Some of them viewed with irritation the condemnatory attitude expressed by Cardinal Basil Hume of Westminster who on the one hand condemned such self protective measures by Irish people and on the other advocated the keeping of nuclear weapons by the British government because of their deterrent value.

A group of West Belfast residents made these issues known to the Mitchell Commission in the following submission:

1. Catholics have been attacked on average once every twelve years in major pogroms. These uprisings against the Catholic population were fomented by preachers, politicians and secret societies led by clergymen. During the pogroms the mobs were often led and seldom hindered by the RUC.

The purpose of these regular pogroms was to drive Catholics out of areas where their vote could have changed the electoral pattern, and to reduce Catholic political, economic, or cultural influence or power. Areas in East Belfast and North Belfast were denuded of most of their Catholic population in this readjustment of voting patterns to ensure that government control was maximised.

There is no evidence that sectarian hatred is itself the primary motive factor in initiating such attacks. Government policy of retaining territory at all costs is the primary factor.

Catholic people must be protected – and if necessary equipped – to ensure that this never happens again.

**2.** When the IRA disarmed or was disarmed in the past, these pogroms against the Catholic population inevitably followed. In the 1920s when the republican movement was defeated pogroms against the Catholics were extremely severe, so much so that even church leaders who normally kept silent, protested internationally. In the 1930s when there was no protection the same happened. In the 1960s the republican movement voluntarily gave away its arms in order to engage in purely agitational and non-military politics. By 1969 the houses were burning, Catholics were killed, the non-military Civil Rights movement had been beaten into the ground and thousands of refugees were streaming out of their homes in Belfast and elsewhere.

The lesson is clear – whatever people think of the IRA, every time the IRA disarms the pogroms recommence. If the IRA is forced to disarm now the same will happen again unless a superior force prevents it.

**3.** When Catholics were attacked they appealed for help. The British government, whose agents fomented the attacks, did not intervene to help the Catholics, instead, allowed the police to attack them and later the military attacked them also.

They appealed to the Dublin government in 1969–70 and were promised weapons to defend themselves. The Dublin government gave some people training in the use of weapons and moved some of its own weapons and army up as far as the border. Then it gave instructions that no weapons were to be given to the men they were training and that their own army was to go no further than the border, and finally arrested the men, including cabinet ministers and one of their own army officers whom they had instructed to provide for the defence of Catholics in the six counties.

The churches refused to do anything effective to protect the people but insisted on them taking down their makeshift barricades to let the police and British army into areas from which the people in terror had excluded them.

The US government refused to act, so did European governments, the Vatican kept silent throughout and even in 1979 refused to have the pope even visit the area although asked to do so by Catholics and Protestants alike.

In view of this it is totally unacceptable that Catholics should be asked to depend upon the protection of the Dublin and London governments, the churches, other governments, or the police. Some protection must be available which is independent of – and even punitive towards if necessary – all of these.

**4.** If adequate protection is not available for Catholics, they are morally justified in providing for their own protection from now onwards.

Further, if protection is not available from those whose duty it is to protect citizens, Catholics are not only justified but are morally bound to protect their families and homes and to create and use whatever means are necessary to that end.

However, such problems could have been prevented and present problems resolved if the British government had made an internationally enforceable undertaking that it will never attack Catholic people here again. It has refused to do this. Such an undertaking would have made it possible for those of us who are not attached to political parties and have watched the attacks on our people for decades to advise some means of decommissioning weapons. Without such an internationally enforceable undertaking that our homes are never going to be violated again, such advice about decommissioning of weapons is impossible and, arguably, immoral. It is immoral to allow people to be attacked again and again and again.

In no circumstances should the British government be allowed to enforce decommissioning of weapons because the probable consequences are too grave. If it is willing to make an internationally enforceable declaration of non-aggression towards Catholics, the problem can be solved and weapons can be removed from the scene. If it is not willing to do this then the weapons of the IRA cannot be decommissioned because the risks are too great.

**5.** The British government has the power to remove most of the weapons from our society and has refused to do so. It has the power to put under guard all police and British army weapons, to revoke all licences for guns and renew them under strict conditions, and to stop the flow of illegal weapons through their intelligence services and other forces to their supporters. They also have enough knowledge concerning the whereabouts of illegally held weapons to call them in and deal with them. All this they have refused to do. In the absence of such action on their part, no decommissioning of other weapons should be discussed. The risks to the Catholic population are too great.

**6.** The objective of the armed strategy of the British government has always been to reduce the economic, political and military power of Catholics with a view to holding territory in Ireland. Since it still wishes to hold the territory it must be assumed from this that it is willing also to use all the methods it used in the past – keeping the Catholic population at a manageable level of one-third, as in the 1920s, or to reduce it to that level if it tends to increase – as they attempted to do in 1969 and later, and restricting Catholics to certain areas where they will not unduly influence the pro-union vote.

It has to be recognised that the problem is not one of Protestant-Catholic relationships but one of government intent upon holding territory by whatever means are necessary including forceable reduction of the Catholic population. This has been government policy in the past and there is no evidence that the policy has changed or is going to change.

An alternative British government strategy is to induce a sizeable portion of the Catholic population to support the union and this has met with only moderate success, as the smallness of the Alliance Party and the minority support of pro-union policies within the SDLP have shown. If such a strategy were successful there might be some hope that reduction and control of the Catholic population would no longer be seen as necessary to the government. But even if a sizeable portion of the Catholic population were won over now, there is no guarantee that these will remain in support of the union if, as is likely, economic advantage will be available to them under another political arrangement, for example a united Ireland.

Rather than rely upon the support of Catholics who might favour the union, the British government is likely either to revert completely to the policy of reducing the political and economic power of the Catholics and/or reducing the Catholic population to manageable proportions as the occasion demands. They may try to carry out such a strategy with the help of those Catholics who favour the union.

7. The intervention of the European Union or the United States, while desirable, is not sufficient to guarantee the safety of the Catholics in the six counties. What the EU and USA require is trade and, for trade, stability. Stability can be achieved by oppressive government, and trade may well flourish at the expense of democratic government. The six county state was designed as a one-party state, with no possibility of changing the government by democratic means. For many years there was stability but this was achieved in such a way that a Civil Rights movement was necessary and inevitable, and when this movement was frustrated and beaten down by government, an armed revolution was inevitable. If we try to get stability for trade at the expense of justice for all the people we will fail, and war will become inevitable in the future even if superior

force may prevent or stop it now.

**8.** No one in the six counties has sufficient reason to trust government. Government must be made to face this reality and to create a just society even against its will. The British system is not a modern democratic one, even in Britain and therefore to produce a democratic system in Ireland would be extremely difficult for the London government without creating a constitutional problem in Britain itself. This reality has to be taken into account and we have to ensure that the difficulties in making a settlement are not laid at the door of citizens, whether armed or not, who did not create the undemocratic situation which existed for the past 70 years.

On no account should the Commission help to give the impression that the minor problem of decommissioning is a major problem, and that therefore the inability of the British government to create a democratic system need not be discussed.

The London government which created the problem has a primary responsibility to cease from aggressive propaganda against the Catholic and Protestant population which accuses them of having created the problem when in fact they are both victims of it. A primary duty of the British government is to enter into talks at once with all elected representatives while consulting with all unelected people who have an interest or who have power in the situation. Until April 1995 the British government had never in our history conceded that all Irish Catholics had a right to elect their representatives and be heard through them. They finally conceded the principle but clearly they are intent upon delaying as long as possible the implementation of it. This, and not the fear of IRA weapons, seems to be the reason for their delay in holding talks with those elected to represent the wishes of the people.

**9.** In view of the above we recommend that:

**a)** On no account should the Commission recommend any group to disarm unless and until the British government makes an internationally enforceable guarantee that it will never attack Irish people and in particular Irish Catholics again either directly or through its agents. Such a declaration can be made, if the government wishes, in a formula which would be clear and unambiguous but at the same time would not unduly embarrass the government.

**b)** The Commission should recommend that the best and only way to decommissioning is through talks involving all the elected representatives of the people and that without such talks decommissioning is dangerous and futile.

**c)** The Commission should publicly recognise that all weapons must be included in discussion – it is wrong for the government to say that their army or police weapons are different from those of armed citizens' groups – if the weapons are used to kill civilians then they are the same, and should be treated as the same.

If we use the formula that it is not the weapons but the use of the weapons that must be decommissioned then we allow both government and citizens' military groups some room to move.

The government have to agree – with adequate means to enforce the agreement – that while it is allowed to keep its weapons it must be prevented from using them for killing civilians, while citizens' military groups must agree that their weapons will never again be used. Both sides are agreeing exactly the same thing and neither is shamed.

**d)** If the two governments insist absolutely on decommissioning, as the British government understands it, as a precondition to talks, the recommendation should be made that there should be no talks. The risks are too great.

If the British government refuses to make an internationally enforceable declaration that it will never attack our people again and if the IRA and other groups make any move towards decommissioning, however slight that move may be, then Catholics must be encouraged to apply for personal weapons to protect themselves if necessary, and must be given the assurance that such applications will be examined and approved by an authority independent of the British government, and that if appeal to the European courts for the right to such personal protection is necessary, such appeal should be facilitated by the Dublin government and not impeded by the London government.

Their submission was ignored.

It was only in the aftermath of the Orange Order's programme of disruption and defiance of the police and government at Drumcree in July 1996, the murder of Michael McGoldrick and the eviction of many families from their homes that some journalists recognised the validity of what the West Belfast residents had said to the Mitchell Commission, that the protection of the Catholic population would be in danger if the IRA decommissioned:

> John Major spent 17 months squandering an opportunity to build a lasting peace in this island. He did this, primarily, by demanding that the IRA surrender its weapons. Even someone of Major's limited intelligence would hardly make such a request of the IRA leadership in the wake of last week's violence ... ( Editorial, *Sunday Business Post*, 14 July 1996)

> A few months ago at a rally Gerry Adams said, 'The IRA haven't gone away, you know'. And we all agreed, how misguided, how pointless, how foolish. But for a few hours on Thursday night, when things looked as black and white as they ever did on our old television in 1972, I hoped to God he was right. (Brenda Power, *Sunday Tribune*, 14 July 1996).

# 5

# NON-SECTARIAN MURDER

It was clear by the mid 1970s that many killings in the six counties described as 'sectarian murders' were not sectarian. Many of them were committed by British intelligence agents directly or through others recruited from the Protestant or Catholic population and by the SAS (Special Air Service) which had used the same methods already in Malaysia, Oman, Yemen and later in the Falklands/Malvinas conflict. The Miami Showband murders, directed by a Benedictine-educated British agent, Nairac, was one of the crudest examples of such killings.

In the 1970s members of loyalist, republican and nationalist groups in Belfast kept contact with each other. None of them wanted a sectarian war into which these falsely named 'sectarian killings' were planned to lead them. Republicans had no interest in a sectarian war; their objective was to attack British government operatives, whether these were Catholic, Protestant or other; loyalists killed not for simply sectarian reasons but as part of a coolly worked out political strategy to remove Catholics from certain electoral areas, to make Catholics in general afraid, thus putting pressure on the IRA to cease its operations, and eventually to remove specific political opponents. These were political aims and sectarianism was not a primary motive in the killings but gave them cover and helped to make them more easily possible. Sectarian killings did occur, the killers motivated by propaganda rather than political reason but these were probably relatively few.

The description of political killings as 'mindless' and 'senseless' is misleading. In a political conflict few actions are mindless but describing them as such diverts attention from real causes so that government, political parties and others do not have to discuss them. Anti-Catholic pogroms have a political purpose, assassination has a political purpose. Innate Protestant hatred of Catholics is the primary motive cause of neither. Induced hatred is an instrument used to bring them about for political gain.

One of the major difficulties in assessing the six county situation is the refusal of commentators to attribute rationality to Irish people, whoever they may be. Nationalists and republicans, unionists and loyalists are described as acting for tribal reasons, or through instinct or because of deep seated prejudices which they are incapable of resisting. If these assessments are true, all those brought before the courts for political offences should be released or given lesser sentences because of diminished responsibility. Unionists or loyalists may be, but nationalists and republicans seldom are; they may instead be given more severe sentences because their offence, whatever commentators say about its motivation, is recognised by the judges as political. The myth persists that what is done by people in the six counties is not motivated by reason but by hatred, prejudice, enslavement to history or fear of reprisals. That people should have a more or less carefully worked out reason for doing what they do, whether it is voting, supporting revolution, marching in the streets or opposing those who march is not thought worth serious consideration. Killings are described as mindlessly sectarian when the evidence shows they are not. People who have made costly decisions to live in mixed areas are accused of not being able to live at peace when they are driven out. The real political and economic reasons for what the secret societies, business people, politicians or churches do are ignored as the explanation of tribal hatred is less demanding. That British intelligence agents killed for political reasons and pretended the killings were sectarian has been documented by writers including some of the British agents themselves, for example Holroyd and Wallace.

Such so-called sectarian killings were carefully crafted political acts to inflame conflict between Protestants and Catholics and for other political reasons. This was known to the Dublin and London governments and to church leaders; a constant flow of information went to them from the six counties which said so, but the myth persisted that the main problem in the six counties was sectarianism and the killings a result and proof of it.

> ... despite almost two years of relative peace, the 'tribes' of Northern Ireland remain very far apart. There has been much wishful thinking since 1994 that because of the reduction in violence the problem has in essence been solved. The fact, however, is that the IRA and the UVF were never the cause of the problem. Rather they were the malignant manifestation of a bitterly divided society.[1]

The myth expressed here is that undemocratic government is not the principal cause of the six county disaster or even the armed groups. It is the people who refuse to adjust their tribal life even when it causes death. This myth has persisted, not because all the people believe it but because it is fostered by governments, journalists, church officials and others who encourage people to engage in community relations activities which cannot change the situation but give those engaged in them, as well as those who finance and encourage them, a sense of purpose but no incentive to make real change.

While British agents were developing the pattern of 'sectarian killings' they also set up brothels, vice rings and businesses. Kincora Boys' Home was one unit of one vice ring. Vice rings were in operation between Belfast, Mid-Ulster, Dublin and London along which young men and boys were passed for use by army officers and others. Information about these rings was available to governments and church officials but they were allowed to go on relatively unhindered. Robert Bryans in his *The Dust Never Settled* describes the British and Irish setting in which such vice rings existed among political and church people even in times of peace.[2] Fr Peter McVerry, SJ, said in Dublin that a vice ring was being used by, among others, army officers. His statement was received with coolness.

Observers in the six counties understood why neither state nor church authorities often pursued such matters. In the six counties complaints were made but soon died away because they received little support even from those who were normally critical of sexual indulgence of any kind. Paddy Devlin, trade unionist and public representative tried to make the authorities close massage parlours which sprang up from the beginning of the increased military presence in the six counties. He failed.

The attitude of church officials was summed up in a remark made by a Protestant clergyman at a meeting with Catholic clergy in early 1970s. Such meetings between clergy, like communication between political groups, were frequent during the 1970s although propaganda said that Catholics and Protestants could not communicate with each other. A senior Catholic cleric, Canon Pádraig Murphy, remarked to the meeting that church people should do something about the increasing number of massage parlours and similar places being opened in Belfast. One of the Protestant clergy replied that unfortunately they would be there as long as the military were. Murphy interpreted this as meaning simply that soldiers beget brothels wherever they go, but it later appeared more likely that the remark meant the military had to use these as part of their political strategy. They used them to entrap politicians and others who could be enticed to visit them.

Fred Holroyd claimed that when he was working for British intelligence in the 1970s he ran a pseudo-loyalist group in Craigavon, a few miles south of Belfast and at the same time a pseudo-republican group in North Antrim. He was one of a number of such operators. A pseudo-republican group in North Antrim killed a popular Catholic policeman. This killing would, it was hoped, turn public opinion against the IRA by showing it was ruthlessly cruel even towards Catholics. Holroyd denied however that his pseudo-groups committed atrocities against 'their own people', that is, against military and police.

'Sectarian killings' were designed to give the impression that Catholic/Protestant hatred was the main problem in the six counties and that the British government had to refuse democracy to the people because they were incapable of practising it. The same arguments had been used against any people who claimed independence during the days of the British empire. Republicans had to be seen as extremist criminals spawned from a community incapable of living at peace with Protestant neighbours, while loyalist groups had to be seen as a natural expression of Protestant hatred of Catholics. By organising and carrying out the killings the government strengthened its propaganda about Catholic/Protestant antagonism and at the same time helped to create it.

Although neither Catholic nor Protestant communities as a whole wanted sectarian hatred the propaganda was made to come true. The IRA, unwilling to engage in a sectarian war insisted that it was fighting against the British government and its agents, whoever they might be. If however they could be forced to retaliate by killing Protestants as such they would be in a sectarian war whether they willed it or not. The assassination of Catholics would put pressure on the IRA either to get into a retaliatory sectarian campaign or stop the war altogether since the price in Catholic lives would be too high. Whatever happened the government would win. In time however the British government seems to have given up the expectation that the IRA would be goaded into a purely sectarian war. The importation of an exceptionally large consignment of arms from South Africa led to a stepping up of the government's other strategy of putting pressure on the IRA by killing more Catholics. The decision of the IRA not to respond in kind even after the Ormeau Road killings, when five Catholics were killed in a bookmaker's office, showed that the republican policy was going to hold. From this point the assassination of Catholics was not so much to foment sectarian war as to force the IRA to cease its operations because of the number of uninvolved Catholics who would be killed if they did not.

The British government and others insisted that loyalist killings were a reaction against the IRA and therefore their killings would cease if and only if the IRA campaign ceased. When the IRA ceasefire was announced in August 1994 the loyalist ceasefires soon followed. Protestant hatred of Catholics then was clearly not the uncontrolled constant motive factor of killings after all. The 'sectarian' killings could be effectively turned on and off at will. People who burn their neighbours' homes because they hate them do not behave with such discipline. Political operatives do.

If the war resumes it is likely that killing Catholics will again be part of British strategy.

Discussions in the 1970s between unionists and loyalists, nationalists and republicans, Catholics and Protestants took place in different parts of Ireland, in Britain, Holland and the United States. They were wide ranging and sometimes radical. Loyalists discussed different forms of government, government devolved to local communities and local community development. The topics and people involved at that time were similar to those involved in discussions after the ceasefires in 1994.

At some point in the 1970s loyalists were persuaded that such talking was not useful, and that planned killing of Catholics was the most productive way forward for them. Loyalist groups responded and killing of politically uninvolved Catholics increased again. After the ceasefires of 1994 and the political discussions which followed, an important question then was whether loyalists could be persuaded again, as they were in the 1970s, to stop the talking and start a programme of killing again.

There was reason to believe that loyalists would not give in to such persuasion as easily as they had in the 1970s. Many of them had gone to prison and while there asked and answered questions as to why and by whom they had been given this reward for doing what they had been advised to do by politicians whom they trusted too easily and who were all the time rich and free. It would not be as easy in the 1990s to persuade them to stop talking and start killing again as it had been 20 years earlier. But no one, not even they themselves, knew whether their determination not to fight other people's wars, to put Paisley, Smyth, Trimble or the Northern Ireland Office into power, would be strong enough to stop it happening. The answer to the question lay in the minds not only of the loyalists but of British intelligence services.

Rev. Roy Magee, a Presbyterian with close contacts with loyalist leaders, said on 1 May 1996 that some prosperous unionists were trying to undermine the ceasefire. If they were, the determination of active loyalists to be their own masters would be tested. The attempt to persuade them would follow the pattern of such attempts throughout the history of the six county state. Academics, clerics, business people and politicians successfully persuaded those who were less well off, less academically favoured and less influential to fight their battles for them, while they remained clothed in the respectability which, like the war, they created and paid for. After the ceasefires in 1994 an important question was whether they could still do it. Roy Magee's statement suggested that they would still try.

If the loyalists returned to armed activity against Catholics as such it is not certain that the IRA would still have a policy of not replying in kind. Republican men and women who were active in the 1940s and 1950s were among those who had a moderating influence on IRA campaigns – there were certain things they would not approve. But in view of the policy of the British government to use the killing of uninvolved Catholics as a military and political tactic there could be a strong lobby within the republican community saying they had no alternative to fighting fire with fire. Those who would envisage this approach would argue that only this would stop a government which used torture, shoot-to-kill policies, abuse of prisoners, breaking of promises and the killing of uninvolved people for political reasons. The implications of such a decision are clear as the possibility of a civil war rather than a guerrilla war would increase.

There has been no occasion in the history of the six county state when loyalists as such united and fought unless they had the state's police or military in front of them. One of the most daunting tasks of loyalist leaders then as they felt the grip of the once imperial government in Ireland weaken was to persuade themselves and their followers that they could still fight if they were left to themselves. A member of the British government's advice that the British government 'should arm the Protestants to the teeth and get out' indicated that one day indeed they might. Reginald Maudling seriously considered the same possibility. Well armed by the British government they would face into a long and bitter war which they could only doubtfully win.

A reasonable option would be to seize territory, perhaps in east Antrim and use it as a bargaining counter. This could be a relatively danger-free operation. The police and the British army would not interfere, Dublin could not and neither would the IRA. Loyalists, including members of local councils, experimented successfully with closing roads and access to Larne Harbour. The nearby electricity generating station has been controlled by loyalists for a long time.

They needed to be sure however where the loyalties of their members in politics, church, police or army would lie if there were a real confrontation with the British government. The events of Drumcree in July 1996 were an experiment by which they tried to find out. The call went out for organisation through the Orange lodges and for police to refuse to interfere. Both were successful. It was made clear to the British government that while they seemed to be holding the IRA at bay loyalist paramilitaries might intervene and in that case the government would have to oppose them also. British officials had said since the 1970s that if this happened the government would have little alternative to withdrawing. The threat was successful. The demands of the Orange Order were conceded and their efforts to paralyse a significant area of the six counties unhindered.

The one element missing in the Drumcree experiment was the co-operation of the loyalist armed groups. With their armed strength, the Orange Order's organisational ability, British refusal to intervene, seizure of roads and facilities, and Dublin government timidity, the loyalists could make a bid for power which would have been more effective than any in the past 25 years. The absence of support from all the paramilitaries except one group led by Billy Wright, later disowned, was a serious weakness.

Unofficial loyalist citizens groups are of three kinds: those which grew from within a local Protestant population and were later infiltrated by British agents; those set up directly by British intelligence agents; and those which grew up within the Protestant community and were relatively free from British intelligence infiltration.

One of the loyalist organisations set up by British intelligence was the Red Hand Commando, led during some of its most vicious periods by John McKeague. McKeague favoured an independent 'Ulster', or independent six counties as the best structure for six county Protestants. As he became aware of real British attitudes to Irish loyalists he was prepared to say that some structure should be found in which they would be free of both London and Dublin. According to his own account he became aware of real British attitudes when he was interned without trial – one of the few loyalists who were – in Long Kesh. He considered himself a military officer and while in Long Kesh was accompanied by a 'batman' just as British army officers were.

One day he had a meeting with a British army officer. Both were accompanied by their 'batmen'. During their conversation the British officer hit McKeague and knocked him to the ground. It was at that moment, he said, that he realised what the British thought of loyalists. They were little different from the Catholic Irish.

Since McKeague was the leader of a group set up by British intelligence who directed him and in return were told everything significant that was said even in private meetings with him, it is difficult to assess from what he said and did what his real political views were. He was compromised in too many ways to be free to do and say what he wished.

He did however express a current loyalist idea of freedom. Loyalists do not usually talk of freeing themselves from anything, because they have been persuaded that they already have all the freedom they or others should want. Some, like McKeague, wanted to be free of British domination under which they felt reasonably safe but often humiliated, and yet to be free of minority status in an Ireland which they had been taught from childhood to fear. An independent [six county] Ulster seemed a reasonable solution. Loyalists discussed the possibility. Some Catholics discussed it with them because they were dismayed that in some respects the political regime being constructed by Irish people in the south was little better than the one which had been imposed upon the Irish people in the six counties by force. A significant measure of independence could reassure both parties that they would have some control over their own future.

Breaking away from British government domination would be possible but difficult. John McKeague said: 'The Taigs (Catholics) will never get rid of the Brits by themselves, and the Prods (Protestants) will never get rid of the Brits by themselves, but by God when the two of them get together the Brits won't have a chance'. This echoed what British officials and military were saying in the early 1970s, that if they were attacked on two sides they would have to move out. It was essential for the British government that this should not be allowed to happen. The unionist regime had required forcible separation of the Catholics from Protestants, the British military needed it too. It could be achieved by propaganda and if necessary by assassination. In spite of the views he expressed about freedom McKeague became part of the government apparatus of both propaganda and assassination.

British strategy was to defeat the IRA, dissolve the republican movement, win over some Catholics to the union, render the rest politically and economically powerless and ensure that the loyalists were kept under control and did not take to the streets in disaffection against police and military. It was a variation of the strategy described by the English spy, Peter Wright, which was tried in Cyprus:

> The entire Cyprus episode left a lasting impression on British colonial policy. Britain decolonised most successfully when we defeated the military insurgency first, using intelligence rather than force of arms, before negotiating a political solution based on the political leadership of the defeated insurgency movement, and with British force of arms to maintain the installed government. This is what happened in Malaya and Kenya, and both these countries have survived intact. The fundamental problem was how to remove the colonial power while ensuring that the local military forces did not fill the vacuum.[3]

One of the difficulties in creating an Irish democracy in the six counties was that British governments' estimates of their own capabilities had not realistically developed for half a century. Letting controlled loyalist groups loose on Catholics was a tactic in their strategy of management. People like John McKeague were useful when controllable, but expendable always. He was assassinated in January 1982 in his printing shop, unprotected by those whom he had served.

If there was to be a United Ireland – and some unionists realised it would happen – McKeague said he wanted people in the six counties to enter such as union as free people: 'Even if we were independent only from midnight until five past we would at least go into a united Ireland as a free people, we would not be getting forced into it. We would be making our own decisions'.

One of the difficulties to be overcome if the six counties were to be independent was the inability or unwillingness of its rulers to create a viable independent economy. They had preferred to remain subsidised under British rule making no provision for what would happen if a British government decided that remaining in control was not worth their money. They made no realistic attempt to be self-sufficient or even to pay their way within the British economy. To have done so could have weakened the case for Britain staying in power. An independent six counties would need the goodwill and co-operation of neighbouring states but successive governments in Belfast had rejected whatever gestures of goodwill had come from the south and made demands on the British government which in modern times would not be matched by strategic or economic advantages to the government. The homework was not done nor the efficiency attained which would have made independence a realistic choice. A period of democratic rule with equitable economic development could have helped towards encouraging independence but there was no sign of British government willingness to create it. There had been no substantial advance in Civil Rights since the imposition of direct rule in 1972.

For nationalists and republicans however the response to those who suggested an independent state for the north-east was clear: 'You had virtual independence for fifty years and abused it; we cannot risk the same again'. Unionists' fear of nationalists and republicans stemmed from what they might do; nationalists and republicans feared the unionists because of what they had already done.

It was always difficult to assess the political views of loyalists, including John McKeague because so many of them were not their own masters. British intelligence agencies had too great a hold on them and they might therefore be laying false trails to give a misleading impression of what the British or their loyalist allies were thinking. However, since what Mc-Keague was saying was similar to what some members of the Ulster Defence Association were saying it probably reflected accurately the thinking among a significant number of loyalists during the 1970s.

Like all solutions proposed by Irish people that of independence for the north-east was not allowed to be officially discussed as a possibility. It was made clear by Dublin and London that only the solution proposed by the British, namely rule from Westminster with compulsory power-sharing in a local six counties devolved government could be discussed. This was the one solution which no group in Ireland, unionist or nationalist, had proposed but was the only one they were allowed to negotiate about.

John McKeague was assassinated shortly before he was to be questioned in a child abuse investigation. The man accused of killing him was a republican but the killing was convenient for those, including British intelligence agents, who could not afford to have evidence given in court such as John McKeague might provide.

# 6

# TORTURE INTENDED

The Stormont and Westminster governments had attacked the Civil Rights movement in the 1960s, and together with the Dublin government and the churches prevented Catholics under attack from getting arms to protect themselves. It was inevitable that a revolutionary force would emerge which would know how to get guns and use them. If the Dublin government had insisted that weapons for defence should be made available to citizens under attack and if the Catholic church had brought its international influence to bear a different situation would have developed. An international crisis would have been caused by any overt interference by the Dublin government and the Vatican would have been required to recognise what it had ignored for decades, that members of the Catholic Church were being subjected to a regime which if it had been ruled by Communists would have been answered by prayers, money and pressure against the government organised from Rome. As it was, the Vatican was content to support the British government in Ireland in exchange for British support for Catholic schooling and for Vatican influence in Europe. There was no Lach Walesa and Solidarity in Ireland worth helping with such resources.

When the inevitable revolutionary movement began to emerge at the beginning of the 1970s but while there was still time to bring about change which could have averted war, the Stormont government used the weapon it had used against dissidents in every decade since the foundation of the state, internment of people on police lists without trial or evidence.

Brian Faulkner as minister of home affairs was responsible for internment carried out by military and police in 1971. This internment involved torture and all the information necessary to indicate that it did was available to Faulkner. What he demanded was not internment as it had been known in every decade of the six county state's existence but something which had been perfected by armies, especially paratroopers, in modern wars and involved torture as a necessary part of it.

In the past internment in the six counties meant taking people, mostly men, out of their homes, off the streets and away from political activity which officials said threatened the state. There was cruelty in the arbitrary arrests and in the way they were done but the main purpose was to remove republicans from active politics, or, the government maintained, from military action. The internment demanded by Faulkner and carried out by British paratroopers in 1971 was different.

The pattern had been set by armies in many countries against opponents of government. One of them was the French army in Algeria. The revolution of the Algerian FLN (Front de Liberation Nationale) began in 1954 and ended with Algerian independence eight years later.[1] The French government was under severe pressure from the colons in Algeria and politicians at home to destroy the revolution in its earliest stages before it had time to develop. But police intelligence files in Algeria were out of date and even if the police had been able to bring them up to date with details of present revolutionaries rather than those who had been active years before, it would take too long to satisfy a government which needed quick results and a speedy destruction of the Algerian revolution.

French army paratroopers were instructed to take over from the police, bring the intelligence files up to date, build up a picture of the FLN organisation and quickly mount an offensive to wipe out the revolution before it took hold. Paratroopers invaded police barracks, seized what files there were and took charge of the counter-revolution. The police were angered by this invasion of their territory. The military, finding how inadequate and outdated the files were, carried out a massive arrest operation in which hundreds of people, many of them hardly even on the edges of political activity, were caught and brought to military barracks.

The military were interested in hard information from people deep inside the FLN but also in peripheral information from people who knew just what they heard in the cafes and streets. They tortured those whom they arrested. Information, sometimes from the most marginal of people, was put together until the military had an outline of FLN organisation and people possibly involved in it. Once the gaps were filled in and the picture completed the devastation of the FLN could begin soon and end quickly. Tortures they used included high pitched noise, exhausting posture, sleeplessness, fright, burning over radiators and with cigarettes, beating, near drowning, etc.

This model of arrest, internment and torture used by the French paratroopers in Algeria is the same as that used by the British paratroopers in Ireland when they seized, tortured and interned in 1971. Frs Denis Faul and Raymond Murray listed 25 principal methods of torture used in Holywood and Girdwood barracks. They included heavy punching, beating with batons, kicking, putting men over hot radiators, beating on the head, hand squeezing of testicles, insertion of instruments into anal passage, injections, electric cattle prodding, electric shocks, burning, deprivation of sleep, urinating on prisoners, use of amphetamine drugs, Russian roulette, etc., etc. [2]

Peripheral as well as hard information was important to the British military and police; very few IRA members were caught, but that did not mean that other people were useless to the information gatherers. Peripheral information was so valuable that they tortured to try to get it.

The French/Algerian model had been a matter of public knowledge for years and was accepted by the British military and their government as a proper tactic to use in Ireland. It had evoked a fierce controversy in France as the French people were shocked that their civilisation and moral code could be set aside by politicians and military to admit torture for any reason.

Similar techniques of torture as those used by the French were taught to police and military in Britain before and during the internment period in the six counties (1971–1974). The best documented legal evidence that terrorism and torture were carried out in Ireland on instructions from the British government was presented by the Irish government in the European court. It dealt with the torture and ill treatment of men arrested in the six counties on internment day, 9 August 1971. It was established in that court that RUC officers had been selected for, and underwent training in techniques which were illegal and used on selected internees. The training was carried out in military bases in England. The British government was found guilty but the RUC officers who had violated the European Convention on Human Rights had no charges brought against them.

Faulkner insisted that the internment operation be carried out by the British army and RUC. The implementation of the plan was left to the military. By doing this, Faulkner knew, or ought to have known, that this would inevitably result in abuse of the prisoners – to that extent he was responsible for the torture that ensued. He did not at any time express regret or hesitation about the techniques used nor did he try to stop or mitigate them. He signed the order for every victim who was seized and interned. When he spoke of internment he said it was to remove IRA gunmen from the streets, thus invoking the rationale of previous internments and disregarding the systematic torture for information which was a new and now accepted element in it. Even if he had not known at first what internment by the military involved, he would know soon after the operation began and still did nothing to stop it. Information that men were being tortured was available to the public within a week of the first arrests.

The Algerian experience had shown that allowing paratroopers to move the police aside and take charge of information gathering made torture inevitable. It had become normal paratrooper method.

Some Church leaders did not object to internment being imposed. The government in Dublin did not condemn internment as such but deplored the political poverty which inspired it in the six counties. Dr James Haire of the Presbyterian Church accepted it. George Otto Simms, Archbishop of Armagh and some other clergy accepted it also:

> We recognise that because of the continuing violence and bloodshed for which there can be no Christian justification the Government in its duty to all citizens has no option but to introduce strong measures which must be distasteful to many.

> We regret the necessity for the introduction of internment. We note however that there is already provision for an Appeals Committee. This is designed to safeguard the rights of law abiding citizens ...[3]

This statement, according to Eric Gallagher and Stanley Worrall, was made to placate church members who demanded it.[4] There is no evidence to indicate that it did not represent also the views of the leaders who made it.

Cardinal Conway was persuaded to fly to London, reluctantly, to complain not about internment but about abuses which he had been persuaded accompanied it. His protest and the approval of internment by the other church leaders overlooked the fact that torture was a necessary part of the process ordered by Faulkner and not an act of casual cruelty that happened by accident or was carried out by a few 'bad apples'. A few clerical voices were raised in protest. Fr Brian Brady declared internment without trial immoral even before news of the torture reached the public. So did the Civil Rights Association. The battle lines were being drawn between those who believed that morality must be defined by civil and church authorities and those who believed it must be defined first of all not by those who watched but by those who suffered. The tensions between the two were to appear often during the next 25 years.

The British government said later that what they did to prisoners was not torture because the people engaged to do it did not take pleasure in it. Whether they took pleasure in it or not was irrelevant. They did what Faulkner and the British government intended, tortured men in order to get political information. Political and clerical approval of the internment process remained strong even as information became increasingly available of prisoners being tortured. Four years later, in 1975, after internment had been 'phased out' to be replaced by other forms of imprisonment with a minimum of evidence, an Anglican Church working party announced its disapproval of internment.

The government in Dublin could not condemn internment

because they might use it themselves in the future. Of the 69 governments which according to Amnesty International use torture for information a substantial number govern countries with Catholic majorities. Religious considerations in the Republic or elsewhere would not necessarily inhibit it. If a Dublin government used internment without trial in its own territory it might or might not use the same model as the French in Algeria and the British in the six counties. There is no evidence to suggest they would not. Within the police (gardaí) in the south a core group emerged in the early 1970s who had the reputation of getting results and not being too fussy about how they got them. Suspects alleged they were physically and otherwise abused. They were known as the Heavy Gang.[5] The existence of this gang was commented on by the Dublin government after the IRA ceasefire in 1994 when it seemed that their existence would no longer be an issue. Since then there have been further allegations of ill-treatment by suspects in custody.

When the military and police in the six counties had gained as much information as they were likely to get from mass arrest, torture and internment the government became tolerant of a political movement to get rid of it. When internment without trial was phased out at the end of 1975 however it was replaced by legal processes which practically ensured that all persons accused of political offences would be jailed. But during the 25 years' war some police and military used torture and mental and physical abuse after they were officially said to have ceased. In 1996 when many of the British military had left the streets the RUC was still using oppressive techniques about which Dr Joe Hendron MP complained in February 1996: 'The RUC have learned how to inflict hurt without leaving a mark ...'

Those who could have protested against the torture/ internment process and did not do so may plead now that they did not know what was going on. But with the French/ Algerian and other models more than 40 years old and information about this and other torture processes available to all in the six counties who wanted to have it, it is difficult to imagine people in Belfast, Bangor, Armagh or Derry not knowing what was happening in military barracks only a few miles from their homes. Similar claims have been made by others – the Nazis had a concentration camp, Dachau, 16 miles from the centre of Munich, Auschwitz a few miles from Cracow and Buchenwald only ten kilometres from Weimar but the people of these cities professed not to know what was happening so near their homes and workplaces. An operation involving thousands of trains, railway and other transport workers – Auschwitz was chosen for a concentration camp because of its railway complex – civil servants, police, soldiers, doctors, industrialists was, they would say, unknown to them all and the 64,000 citizens of Weimar did not know about the 50,000 who are said to have been killed so near them. Whether they knew or not, after the war they were accused of being both aware and guilty:

> The average German had other problems anyway, such as where his next meal was coming from and whether his father or uncle or brother in Russian captivity would ever be released. But if he ventured abroad, he would be unlikely to look you in the eye, because the films about the atrocities of Auschwitz and Belsen had preceded him. He was guilty by association.[6]

In the six county situation all the information necessary to show that prisoners were likely to be tortured was available to those who had demanded arrest and internment by the military. All the information needed to show it was actually happening was available to the public within days. The English *Daily Telegraph* of 18 November 1971 admitted that the precedent for their army's treatment of prisoners in Ireland was that of the Chinese in Korea and the French in Algeria. It was reported on the same day that a member of the British House of Commons said that if torture was not allowed the alternative was equally foolish, namely to ask suspects courteously to help by giving information – some middle way had to be found. Already an answer was being prepared for international consumption which would say that what the British were doing in Ireland was not torture but allowable severe treatment in a crisis. Those in the House who had seen American films depicting 'the third degree', a form of torture for information used in America, would be mentally prepared to accept it. Others might not. Those who learned about the torture in the six counties and wanted it to stop were powerless while the people in power and most of their fellow citizens chose to ignore it. Most of the journalists decided to set the public mind at ease rather than arouse their indignation.

The pattern of the French/Algerian operation was mass arrests, torture of the prisoners, release of those who were un-involved or peripheral, keeping the rest in prison, using the in-formation gathered by torture to bring political files up to date for a speedy attack on the revolutionary organisation and leadership. The operation demanded by Brian Faulkner and supplied by the British military with the agreement, possibly at times reluctant, of the RUC was almost exactly similar.

A significant difference between the Algerian and the British/Irish situation however was the lively and often bitter debate which arose about the general who created the torture in Algeria and the general who resigned rather than counten-ance it. The debate ebbed and flowed around these two men as the French faced their consciences and accepted their failure to keep Algeria even by torturing their opponents.

No such stirring of official consciences has taken place in Britain or Ireland yet.

# 7

# THE CLERICAL STATE

The six county state was supported from the beginning by Protestant clergy. In 1919 a delegation composed largely of clergy – Church of Ireland, Methodist and Presbyterian – was sent to the United States to explain the unionist case. Among the delegates were Rev. Wylie Blue, a Presbyterian Scot ministering in Belfast, Rev. Louis Crooks, an Anglican and another Presbyterian Rev. William Corkey. Their task was 'to explain and justify opposition to the Sinn Féin movement'.[1] This meant explaining and justifying opposition to political change for which the majority of Irish people had voted in the general election of 1918. It meant also explaining and justifying a campaign which included the Solemn League and Covenant of 1912 and the importation of weapons in 1914. The Solemn League and Covenant against Home Rule for Ireland was signed by many clergymen, and weapons imported for the Ulster Volunteer Force in 1914 to oppose it were hidden, among other places, in the home of a Protestant bishop, while bullets were made by volunteers in Protestant church halls.[2] The bishop's house was at Drumalis, near Larne.

The UVF guns were to be used not primarily against Catholics but against the British government if it should continue with plans to give home rule to Ireland. The campaign against home rule then was directed against the decisions of a majority of Irish people, of the British government and of a majority of the elected representatives of the British people, and it threatened armed insurrection if they were put into effect. The clergy who defended this campaign later defended the maintenance of the state of the six counties on the grounds that it was the will of a majority of its people and that change must not be brought about by insurrection or the threat of it.

The strong unionist campaign supported by armed force in the north-east enabled the British government to impose the imperial solution of ceding most of Ireland to a native government while holding on to strategic ports and creating a new six county state with unchangeable government. But once this object was achieved the government had to view with concern the existence of a large militia which, although it was in favour of British control in Ireland, had pledged itself to fight the government if necessary. The government's problem of peacefully dispersing the armed force did not arise however. The UVF were diverted, their purpose in Ireland achieved, to fight not against, but for, the British government and to die in the crassly managed and deliberately wasteful battles of the First World War.

In the south there was a parallel process. The Irish Volunteers were a strongly organised and partly armed counter force to the UVF. As such they supplied a strong arm for politicians. Creating battalions of marching men is a political tactic often designed to strengthen politicians rather than to fight wars. The UVF was not created to fight at the Somme. Perhaps it was not created to fight anywhere. Most of the Irish Volunteers were not allowed to fight in Ireland. The UVF who were sent to fight in France and the Volunteers prevented from fighting at home were not in this situation only because the fight in France was more just or the cause had been won in Ireland. The usefulness of both at home was at an end. Carson wanted a street display, he did not necessarily want a war. MacNeill wanted a street display, he did not want a war at all. If a war was to be fought in Ireland now there would be very few to fight it. Clergy in the six counties as well as politicians who encouraged the formation and aims of the UVF encouraged also their passage to France.

In 1981 a Church of Ireland delegation went to the Episcopal Church in the USA 'to counter propaganda about Northern Ireland' – defence of the regime by clergy had become a permanent and necessary feature of the politics of the six counties. While such Protestant Church delegations defended the regime, the Roman Catholic Church after the first few years of the six county regime officially refused to oppose it, although from time to time it condemned governmental and other abuses.

It may be difficult to understand why church officials or democratic politicians opposed the campaign in the United States for adoption of the MacBride Principles for fair employment. But for the official Catholic Church and the SDLP political change had to come about through them and not through campaigns run by others whose campaigns they did not direct and over whose actions they had no control. The opposition of both to the MacBride and other campaigns is more easily understood in the light of this. Some church and political representatives suggested that these anti-discrimination campaigns were fronts for Sinn Féin or the IRA and that they had little real regard for Civil Rights except as a weapon against the British government. The same had been said about the Civil Rights movement in the 1960s, that the campaigners were really looking not for Civil Rights but for the subversion of the state.

Whereas the churches and conservative politicians had discouraged or disregarded the Civil Rights movement in Ireland they actively opposed the MacBride and other private citizens' campaigns abroad. By the 1980s Catholic clergy were joining Protestant clergy on visits abroad to condemn the IRA and defend the government. A civil servant at the Northern Ireland Office, Margaret Johnston, was ordained by the Presbyterian Church and went on visits to America and Australia, speaking in favour of the government, against the MacBride Principles for Fair Employment and in defence of British governments' human rights record in Ireland, sometimes accompanied by a Catholic priest, Fr Oliver Crilly, a parish priest working in Co. Tyrone. The Irish Catholic hierarchy asked bishops in the USA and elsewhere not to intervene against the policies of the British government although human rights groups asked them to do so.

The support of clergy for the six county regime can be seen in events like these and also in the everyday intercourse between religion and politics – in 1910 Dr William Patterson had the Union Jack permanently floating above his pulpit in May Street Presbyterian church,[3] in 1996 the flag was flying above the Anglican church at Drumcree in Co. Armagh while thousands of Orangemen confronted the police demanding to be allowed march from the church through an area from which Catholic residents wanted them excluded.

Protestant churchmen, unionist politicians and their followers however, in spite of the political and economic favour they enjoyed, regarded themselves as a beleaguered garrison rather than as citizens of a democracy. Some clergy brought in from outside, strengthened their resolve and saved them from becoming an internationally isolated garrison. Few Protestant clergy hoisted the union flag on their pulpits but many flew it outside their churches during the Orange Order celebrations in July and at other times of the year. It was a strange anomaly that Presbyterian clergy should hoist it at all. The Battle of the Boyne which the Orange Order and the churches commemorate resulted in nearly a hundred years' persecution of Presbyterians as well as Catholics, but the need to hold together the uneasy alliance between Anglicans and Presbyterians to form a majority against the Catholics in the six counties required that Presbyterians should be persuaded to believe that the Boyne was a triumph for their religious liberty. If there had not been a need to preserve this alliance it is probable that Anglicans and Presbyterians in the six counties would have been antagonistic to each other on this and other issues and the Orange Order would eventually be understood as an instrument of domination over Presbyterians and other 'dissenters' as well as Catholics.

A sense of superiority is still expressed by the title 'The Church of Ireland' which suggests that other Irish churches do not exist. The Anglican claim to be 'The Church of Ireland' although it is a minority is parallel to the Roman Catholic Church claim to be the one authentic Christian church, whether it is small or large in any place. During discussions about possible ways of creating reconciliation between Christians the leaders of these churches have not indicated willingness to withdraw either of their claims.

Anglicans in Ireland because of their position as the state church under British rule until 1869 were the only Christian body with the legal right to call their places of worship 'churches'. Other Protestants were to be content with worshipping in mission halls, chapels, temples, while the term 'church' was strictly speaking for Anglicans only. No other body was presumed to have use of a 'church'. Catholic churches in the six counties and even in the rest of Ireland are referred to regularly by Protestants and often by Catholics as 'chapels' although this is a reminder of historic inferiority in law. Although in other countries studies have been made of hidden prejudice, that is, of prejudice so interwoven with everyday speech and usage that is it is now active but unnoticed, no such study has been done in Ireland. Everyday prejudice against fellow citizens may be deplored, but is seldom studied. To do so would reveal not only the tragedies it causes but the people and organisations responsible for them. The results of such a study would surprise those who assume that churches are necessarily involved in reconciliation and repentance. In some of them the language of exclusion and contempt is still alive after centuries of Christian living and 25 years experience of revolutionary war:

> The purest churches under heaven are subject both to mixture and error; and some have so degenerated as to become no churches of Christ, but synagogues of Satan. Nevertheless, there shall be always a church on earth to worship God according to his will ...
>
> There is no other head of the church but the Lord Jesus Christ; nor can the Pope of Rome in any sense be head thereof, but is that anti-christ, that man of sin, and son of perdition that exalteth himself in the church against Christ and all that is called God ...[4]
>
> The Cardinal is a red-hatted weasel ...[5]

The six county state's rhetoric of political contempt has deep and perhaps permanent religious roots.

Relations between churchmen and the unchangeable six county unionist governing party however were not always smooth. The first unionist administrations wanted integrated education, to make the separate state more secure and to reconcile Catholics to a regime which, like most of their Protestant fellow citizens, they had not wanted. Presbyterian clergy in co-operation with the Orange Order however, insisted that schools must have bible teaching, and by bible teaching was meant in effect Protestant religious instruction.

This sometimes bitter disagreement between unionist politicians and unionist churchmen on the function and control of schools continued for decades. Protestant clergy threatened to bring down their own government.[6] If the six county government fell it would have meant not a change of party in government, because such a democratic change had been rendered impossible, but a change of personnel within the permanently governing party. This threat was real enough to make the government agree to what the clergy required, and segregated education was inevitable in spite of the wishes of Lord Londonderry, the first minister for education, and some other unionists.

If the Presbyterians had not achieved segregated education the Catholic hierarchy would have done so.

The government minister, Lord Londonderry, who worked towards integration in the 1920s was forced to resign through this pressure from clergy to which the prime minister of the time, Craig, had to submit. Thirty years later the Presbyterian Church forced the resignation of another government minister, R. W. B. McConnell, having given him a severe public rebuke. The rebuke was administered by the Moderator of the time, Alfie Martin – on the liberal wing of Presbyterianism – on the ground that the government had not protected the governor of the six counties, Lord Erskine, his party and members of the church on their way to the opening of the Presbyterian annual General Assembly in 1966. The procession had been threatened and intimidated by Paisley and his followers who had just marched through the largely Catholic Belfast Markets area. After the rebuke by the Presbyterian Church R. W. B. McConnell, minister of home affairs, had to retire from active politics and remained in political obscurity until made a member of the House of Lords nearly thirty years later. McConnell's fault was defined by the Presbyterian Church as failure in his duty of protecting the assembly, not in that of protecting the Catholics whom Paisley was also abusing.

Protestant clergy aided by the Orange Order having insisted on segregation in education were given a large measure of clerical control of the state sector; management committees of state primary schools were required to have at least 50% of their members nominees of the Protestant Churches. In time this right was curtailed by the British government while the Catholic hierarchy was gradually given a unique system of ownership and control of Catholic schools which Protestant Church officials looked upon with some dismay. Protestant leaders in the first two decades of the six county state opted for Protestant clerical control in the state education system because that seemed the best way to keep their influence over education, but by the 1990s their clergy were being edged out of control in the state sector while the Catholics who had opted out of the state system were running what amounted to an education administration system of their own.

While the British government was increasing the Catholic hierarchy's control of education in the six counties the government in the south was trying to reduce it.[7] The British government had become a victim of its own propaganda. In colonial situations it was often assumed that those who controlled the religious leaders controlled the people. St Patrick's College, Maynooth, was set up on this presumption. In a deeply religious society the best controllers of the people were thought to be not police and military but religious leaders. Church or other religious leaders could be favoured while their people were disadvantaged and even persecuted in the belief that control of the people was secure if the bishops and other leaders were kept on the side of the government.

British governments acted on similar presumptions elsewhere. Lord Kitchener and others believed that if they controlled the Islamic religious leaders they could control the Islamic world politically. They failed in both the Middle East and Ireland because when economics and politics demand it, people disobey their religious leaders. Maynooth ordained monarchists and republicans, radical and conservative priests, some for and some against the regimes in which they went to work. However strictly controlled by Catholic bishops, it did not always produce the results governments required. Even when it produced a majority of clergy who supported the British government in spite of its abusiveness, the people in general often disregarded what they preached. Yet the presumption was still alive in the minds of British civil servants and politicians who offered an autonomous education system to the Catholic hierarchy in the six counties with all expenses paid and full ownership of buildings in the hope that in this way they could control the dissent of Catholics. They offered control of development funds for the same reason. In neither case did the policy produce the result the government wanted.

For the churches, control of schools was a matter of power and institutional protection as well as of preserving the ethos of one religious group or another. The schools which were segregated with the stated intention of forming consistently practising Protestant or Catholic Christians did not succeed in doing this. Most adults in the six counties do not attend church consistently, many are even unknown to the churches. In 1996 a Belfast Catholic parish recognised that only 30% of its parishioners had a real attachment to the church, another reported 25%. In a city area described as 'staunchly Protestant' only 20% were known to the clergy or were practising members of any church, and most of the churches depended for their continued existence on those who attended from outside the area. Church attendance and adherence, as in other countries, ceases for most students in six county cities and towns when they leave school. It seems likely that less than half the people of Belfast were baptised into any Christian church.

This was not a new situation. In the 1920s about one-third of its parishioners attended the Rev. Carson's Anglican parish church in East Belfast, an area which has a majority Protestant population. Of the rest some went to mission halls but most went to no place of formal worship. In the 1960s informal observations indicated that in some Catholic parishes about 60% of women and 50% of men were attached to the Catholic church in a vital way. In others about one-third never appeared in church. Thirty years later the numbers had fallen dramatically in a downward movement which was not caused, but may have been accelerated, by the political situation.

Church officials still argue that separate schools are necessary to preserve the ethos of their religious group, although it has been clear for many years that the religious school system does not create adherents or ensure that people will continue to believe in the stated moral code of the churches – teaching about divorce, abortion, sexual relationships, marriage relationships, revolutionary politics and many other things has been given insistently, sometimes aggressively, by the churches but even their practising members often behave differently. All the churches in Ireland opposed divorce at some time. In the six counties it was introduced against the wishes of clergy. The law on abortion was liberalised by the British government against the wishes of the churches. The churches opposed intimate sexual relationships before marriage, extramarital relationships and revolution, but substantial numbers of their members, most of whom were educated in religiously segregated schools, disobeyed their teaching. Preserving the religious ethos through segregated schooling has severe limitations which the proponents of segregation know about but are unwilling to discuss.

Many of those who favour integrated education have said that separate schools cause community divisions which integrated education would prevent or cure. The churches insist, accurately, that separate schooling did not necessarily cause the problem of bad relationships in the state. Some schools and religious groups did set out to cause people to despise each other; most did not. But schools and churches with their enforced separateness helped to create an atmosphere in which others could stir up hatred if they wanted to.

Disdain for fellow citizens of the kind taught in some schools and by some sects should be containable in a normal society just as campaigns like those of Paisley need not have been exceptionally destructive by themselves because any community is likely to have such agitations from time to time. But the six counties was not a normal society in which such abuses would be neutralised or dealt with by law. Catholics could neutralise Paisley's abusiveness by disciplining themselves not to allow it to affect their self-esteem, but the government instead of acting against agitators helped to create and foster them in order to intimidate those who opposed its policies. Abusive opinions about Catholics expressed publicly by government ministers encouraged 43% of Protestants to vote for Paisley during his anti-Catholic campaigns. These campaigns damaged Catholics, but massive Protestant support for them did more than any other factor to put the regime in danger of collapse. As the former prime minister Terence O'Neill put it:

> The future of Ulster was wrecked, not by Treasury meanness, not by lack of forward-looking thinking and planning but by outdated bigotry. We had all the benefits of belonging to a large economy, which were denied to the Republic of Ireland, but we threw it all away in trying to maintain an impossible position of Protestant ascendancy at any price.[8]
>
> So far as Northern Ireland is concerned, she could have continued to enjoy her privileged position of being the only part of Ireland to enjoy a British standard of living. Instead she chose to put all this at risk in the interests of maintaining a Protestant ascendancy that had ceased to have any meaning anywhere else in the United Kingdom.[9]

Integrated education in local schools was not likely to dissolve the power of anti-Catholic campaigns organised outside of them. Nor was it likely to dissolve the racism which O'Neill did not think it necessary to hide even when he was most in favour of reforming the state. When he reflected on what he saw as the defects of the Irish character or said it was 'frightfully difficult' to persuade Irish Catholics to live like Protestants he was indicating a imported racism which integrating local schools in Ballymena and Derry could never dissolve. The roots of racism and opposition to Catholicism were not simply in the uninfluential schools of Ireland but, more significantly, deeply ingrained in the British system where the Eton-educated O'Neill picked it up without recognising it was wrong or knowing that it would one day politically destroy himself and the state of which he was to be prime minister.

If integrated education was to succeed, other, more powerful, institutions which perpetuated racism and contempt needed to be disciplined, their power dissolved. Politicians were unwilling to do this because they would lose votes, churchmen to suggest it because they would lose adherents. It was easier to preach integration to parents and pupils in Irish schools than to attack the racism which had been so normal in English society that when people encountered it in T. S. Eliot, Terence O'Neill, Ronnie Knox or Agatha Christie they did not even realise it was there.

Those in the south of Ireland who insisted that integrated education would solve inter-community tensions in the six counties did not notice that it had not done so in their own state. Their young people were educated in schools where families and descendants of those who fought on the republican side in the civil war sat side by side, played games and learned together with those whose people had fought for the newly formed Free State. Yet in the 1990s it was still said, as Austin Deasy, TD, said in an Easter Sunday broadcast on RTE in 1996, that political parties, voters and others were still affected by the enmities of the civil war. Others put it more bluntly and said the civil war was still being fought out in southern politics. If integrated schooling in the south did not dissolve the enmities of the Irish civil war, it is difficult to argue that integrated schooling would heal the differences between Catholics and Protestants in the six counties. The reality is that there are institutions and associations in both states which powerfully and effectively separate people and artfully make opponents of them, however integrated their children's schooling may be.

These institutions and associations have to be faced and the disintegration they cause has to be acknowledged. If this is done, integration of schools can easily follow and can be effective. Facing them down is difficult because they are powerful. It is easier to campaign for integrated schools as if this were a primary remedy for social, educational, political, economic and military ills which are caused by powerful institutions. Some schools can only with difficulty teach the rudiments of learning, they cannot realistically be expected to solve problems created and perpetuated by the state and the corrosive institutions which control it.

Major problems of poverty, injustice and cruelty in the six county and southern states can continue unsolved while public attention is distracted by less important problems deliberately emphasised to hide the real ones from public scrutiny. The unwillingness of newspaper editors and proprietors to attract and encourage mature commentators is one of the reasons why such distortions can so easily happen. Like undemocratic regimes elsewhere the six county one party state was helped to survive by consenting clergy and journalists.

Most Catholic, Presbyterian, Church of Ireland, Methodist clergy did not campaign against their fellow citizens as Paisley did, but like the schools helped unwittingly to create an atmosphere in which such campaigns could succeed. Separating people in their learning was one way they did it. Directly or indirectly clergy and church based associations inhibited people from inter-marrying, working together, learning together and living in each others' districts. That is, they inhibited people from integrating in the ways most natural to them.

Church leaders opposed what they called 'mixed marriages'. In spite of such opposition as many as 20–30% of Catholic marriages in the six counties were with Protestants or others. Opposition to such marriages was vehement during the early years of the six county state's existence, tended to become less publicly vehement as time went on but remained strong throughout the 25 years of armed conflict. The armed conflict probably did not strengthen or weaken this strongly asserted religious policy. Applicants for admission to the clergy-led Orange Order had to declare that they were from Protestant parents and were either unmarried or married to Protestants. This was an important incentive to avoid 'mixed marriages' because the religious Orange Order had influence over jobs as well as political and other important appointments. Although the advice from churches and the Orange Order was compelling, people went against it. Many of them inter-married in spite of clerical appeals to avoid this most important form of human integration.

People tended naturally to live in mixed districts, going there for work or some other normal reason. This natural integration was practised by the people but frustrated by representatives and activists of churches and church based associations. The twelve year cycles of anti-Catholic attacks which drove people out of mixed areas into one-religion areas were organised largely by religious based secret societies and encouraged by preachers and politicians. The arguments they used to inflame neighbour against neighbour were based on religion. Here again natural and successful integration was frustrated not by the people as a whole but by activists of churches, religious based political parties and secret societies.

Discrimination in jobs and religious harassment of workers were also encouraged by the religious Orange Order, thus frustrating yet another of the people's natural and successful means of integration. Like control of schools and insistence upon segregation in education this was part of a programme of enforced separation. The church based Orange Order also forbade members to drink in Catholic pubs or worship with Catholics in their churches.

While inhibiting integration by these ways natural to the people, politicians and church officials still said they were in favour of integration in a peaceful society and opposed to those who caused conflict. But during the 25 years of war the churches did not lessen their opposition to integration by marriage or shared learning and the Orange Order still opposed mixed housing estates and workplaces. Opposition to inter-marriage was less publicly vehement but just as real as before. Some support was given to the small number of integrated schools created through private efforts but Catholic Church officials refused to provide Catholic chaplains for them and support among Protestant Church people was cool and largely unofficial. The religious secret societies did not alter their policy of forcing segregated housing to control voting patterns. Intimidating people out of mixed areas was still a constant occurrence, reaching a climax in carefully arranged events like the 'siege of Drumcree' when supporters of the Orange Order blocked roads, burned buildings in protest and people were expelled from their homes.

Politicians, church officials and others who inhibited the processes by which people naturally integrate in society did so to ensure that the state, the churches or business would never have to face a combined opposition of Catholics and Protestants who resented low wages, poor working conditions and undemocratic control of their lives. It was easy at any time to break up any informal alliances made by Catholics and Protestants to campaign for better living conditions. Business in the six counties traditionally required a divided community to maintain consistently its lower standards within the British system.

In modern times stability has become more useful to industrialists than politically induced conflict. Mechanisms are available through which workers, employers and governments can agree standards of productivity, wage levels and conditions. Peace became an economic aim rather than conflict as business people insisted that they must use the talents of everyone or fail in a European Community which demands efficiency rather than boasting.

Few political groups in the European Community had boasted so eloquently as the six county unionist parties with so little economic achievement to show for it. Eventually however, business people in the six counties who had supported the unionist regime had to become open to mergers and co-operation and the pursuit of a stable society, even if this meant business relationships with the south which would have been unthinkable a few years previously and pursuit of 'community relations' which in the past many of them had paid to disrupt. Business people in the six counties in the pursuit of prosperity began to become politically independent of preachers and politicians who were willing to sacrifice the prosperity of the whole community to make sure their Catholic fellow citizens would have none of it.

While the churches and their associations inhibited natural integration church officials invented institutional integration. They met each other a number of times each year, held religious services and other inter-community activities many of them funded by the state. While adopting these invented means of integration nothing substantial was done to curb the activities of those whose policy was to destroy any unity such meetings might achieve. The inhibiting of natural integration among the people continued in parallel with attempted integration of the institutions.

The governments in London and Dublin meanwhile continued to insist that the problems of the six counties were due to bad community relations and therefore the main task was not to persuade government to govern differently but to persuade the people to behave better. If they lived together in harmony, they were told, all would be well. The churches, who could find a role in the community relations field but not in creating substantial social or political change, accepted what they described as 'the challenge of community relationships'. The trades unions accepted it also, having avoided the challenge of community relations within the unions for decades in order to keep the trade union organisation intact, although weakened by this policy.

Schools accepted it because they believed they had little alternative, introducing schemes 'for mutual understanding'. Many teachers knew that the analysis on which they were based was false and therefore the solution proposed would be flawed. A Report by the University of Ulster's Centre for the Study of Conflict said that fewer than half of the schools took part in the department of education cross-community contact scheme in 1994–95; only one pupil in nine met a person of another religion on a planned basis; fewer than one in five primary and one in ten secondary pupils were involved; many of the teachers were afraid to broach the subject of religion or inter-community friendships because of the possible reaction of parents.[10] School staffs knew there was little they could do to counter the effects of abusive institutions on children and parents because those institutions are both secret and powerful.

Although the theory that a breakdown of community relations rather than bad government is responsible for the disaster of the six counties, churches, governments and others continue to hold it and continue to spend money on 'inter-community projects' which do not substantially alter the situation. An outcome of this insistence on the primacy of 'community relations' is that initiatives normally accepted as pacifist and non-violent are condemned as if they were immoral. For example when people decided to boycott shopkeepers involved in the Orange Order's practice *coup d'etat* in August 1996, they were rebuked by church leaders and nationalist politicians who argued that anything that disturbed community relations was immoral. Many people decided that their political problems could be solved only by disciplining the members of the secret societies who threatened them and that one non-violent way to do this was to take their custom away from their shops. Others however believed that the secret societies should not be subjected to such a non-violent discipline because fostering good community relations had now been accepted, in spite of its failures and anomalies, as the only way to solve political problems. The community relations theorists held that if the secret societies were treated as if they had done nothing extraordinary they would respond with reason and generosity. There was no evidence, however, that they would.[11]

## STATE CLERGY

After the partition of Ireland Protestant Church leaders had exceptional power in the six counties and Catholic Church leaders had it in the south, power which could be used for good or ill. The political alliance between Presbyterian, Anglican, Methodist and other Protestant groups in the six counties was a successful attempt to contain Catholic power and influence. Catholics in response became a relatively coherent 'minority' while the disparate Protestant groups were held together by a unity of purpose – curbing Catholic power – which usually prevented them from fragmenting and quarrelling among themselves. Serious disruption of this political alliance was caused by the Paisley campaigns against Presbyterians, Terence O'Neill, Chichester Clarke, and other Protestant clergy who were part of the alliance but were opposed by Paisley in his bid for power.

It was difficult for Protestant clergy to speak out for justice or equality or to oppose Paisley's abusive campaigns; the alliance to curb Catholic power must be kept intact and to oppose Paisley or support demands for Civil Rights would split congregations and fragment the alliance. Christians in Ireland then, like Christians elsewhere, kept silent when they could have spoken against oppressive government or religiously motivated abuse. A six county political alliance of the churches prevented Christian witness.

Rev. Carlisle Patterson, a Presbyterian, admitted, 'We cannot evade the truth that for years we have known of various forms of social injustice and political discrimination within our community and that we have found it mentally more comfortable, politically more acceptable and socially more convenient to acquiesce in these things'.[12]

Christian clergy were afraid to speak out against the oppressive preaching and activities of Ian Paisley, who from the 1960s became the most permanently successful of anti-Catholic orators in an area where these had flourished without interruption for more than a century. Clergy, afraid to oppose him individually because they might lose their congregations or their ministries, could not oppose him collectively because their churches were already divided about him. There was no question of the clergy uniting to speak out against religiously induced hatred and suffering the consequences. Churches and their clergy do not as a rule work that way.

When Paisley was agitating in the 1960s he targeted not only the Catholic Church but others as well, especially the Presbyterian Church which he blamed for 'the Romeward trend' he professed to see in it. There was no Romeward trend but the disquiet he caused was so severe that a prominent Presbyterian clergyman Professor John Barkley had to write a booklet to reassure Presbyterians that there was not, while Paisley demonstrated on the streets to protest that there was. Many who joined Paisley's street protest probably did not read John Barkley's pamphlet; it would probably have made little difference if they did.

Between such powerful groups as churchmen and politicians a power struggle is bound to develop in any state. In the six counties the power struggle could be seen in the conflict between government and Presbyterian clergy allied with the Orange Order about education. It was potent although invisible in the hold which the Orange Order, a church based association, had on politicians and others holding important positions in the state. For decades after the founding of the state it was useful to be loyal to the religious Orange Order if one wanted to progress in politics. This struggle for power always simmered beneath the surface but was seldom allowed to emerge clearly into public view because it was believed that Catholic Church leaders would seize whatever advantage such Protestant disunity might offer. Unionist politicians in the six counties had to accept a measure of clerical supremacy in order to get power or to keep it. Nationalist politicians were relegated to a secondary position not only by unionists but also by Catholic Church officials who needed their help but did not want to give them power either.

From time to time the tensions and resentments within the religious/unionist community appeared in the open as during the Paisley march in 1966 against the Presbyterian Assembly. The resulting public rebuke by the Presbyterian Church to the minister of home affairs is notable for a number of reasons. One is that it shows the potential for conflict existing between the traditional unionist family of politicians, business people and clergy on the one hand and the large number of Presbyterians who support Paisley on the other. Also, while political commentators said the south was controlled by bishops it was doubtful if the bishops would have dared summon the government minister responsible for public order to one of their sessions in Maynooth for a public rebuke. That the Presbyterian Assembly should do it in the six counties was so much in keeping with the clerical domination of politics there that it was soon forgotten by the public and the newspapers. Bishop Lucey's dominance would be remembered perhaps forever, while Alfie Martin's would be quietly forgotten.

Alfie Martin, the Presbyterian Moderator at the time of the ministerial rebuke, was a pleasant and companionable man but his demeanour while rebuking McConnell and afterwards showed that he believed a rebuke of a minister of state was within the competence of the Presbyterian Church in the six counties. He did not agree that it should be compared to Catholic bishops in the south summoning a government minister to Maynooth. Not only were the circumstances different, the principles were different also. What was offensive if done by Catholic clergy to a government minister in the south was salutary if done by Protestant clergy to a government minister in the six counties.

Public opinion, in the six counties and the south, as expressed by journalists and politicians has been more favourable to Protestant than to Catholic Church leadership. Protestant Churches are portrayed as liberal in contrast to an authoritarian Catholic Church. Yet Protestant Church leaders and unionist politicians opposed all the liberalising laws proposed in the six counties. They opposed the introduction of the welfare state after the Second World War, a proposed increase in children's allowances, increased financial help for Catholic schools, liberalising laws on divorce, abortion and homosexuality. Liberalising of laws occurred in spite of this through British government intervention but although the clergy wanted a British state they resisted social change which the British government considered necessary for its own people and wanted to extend to the six counties.

When the London government liberalised the law on abortion in 1967 the extension of the law to the six counties was resisted by Protestant clergy. Proposed changes in laws relating to homosexual people were resisted on the streets by demonstrators led by clergymen with the slogan, 'Save Ulster from Sodomy'. Protestant Church and political leaders in their struggle against such liberalising laws were often joined by Catholic colleagues, for example in opposition to the post war welfare state and to liberalising the laws about homosexuality. The myth of Protestant liberalism, however, persisted in spite of the evidence. It was an instrument in a power struggle with the Catholic Church rather than a reflection of the true nature of the Protestant or other Churches.

Their history and origins do not show the Protestant

churches to be more or less liberal than Catholics or others. In the six counties the major Christian groups are built upon models borrowed from outside Ireland, the Catholics on the Roman model, the Church of Ireland on the English, the Presbyterians on a model from Switzerland and Scotland, the Methodists on models from England. There is little left of the earliest forms of Christianity in Ireland since they were submerged and conquered by wave after wave of religious, military and political invasions created and funded by rival Christians. All these rival Christian groups are now in decline and in contention for power in the state and for influence over the faithful.

Individual liberty was not a prominent feature in the history of any of the Christian groups which appeared in Ireland. Calvinist rule in Geneva was of the utmost strictness where citizens were compelled to obey church laws and punished if they did not. Anglican domination in Ireland resulted in persecution of Presbyterians and Catholics. The major Christian churches persecuted those who did not conform to their laws or pay their taxes. Some of their historic leaders were vehement against those who had the misfortune to be racially or religiously different, as Luther was against the Jews:

> First, their synagogues or churches should be set on fire, and whatever does not burn up should be covered or spread with dirt so that no one may ever be able to see a cinder or stone of it ... their homes should likewise be broken down and destroyed, they ought to be put under one roof or in a stable like gypsies in order that they may realise that they are not masters in our land but miserable captives ... We must drive them out like mad dogs.[13]

The ideal of individual liberty in Ireland owes a great deal to the American, French and Irish revolutionaries, little to the Christian churches. It is illogical to attribute an ideal of political, individual and communal liberty to churches which have imposed severe condemnation and penalties on those who refused to join or agree with them until they repudiate the violence which blighted their origins and their history.

At the end of 25 years of revolutionary war the Christian churches in Ireland were officially as strongly against individual freedom of mind, spirit, and choice of political representation as they had been before it. They still opposed liberalising laws, insisted on separate education and worship and still encouraged governments to refuse a hearing to lawfully elected representatives of the people. The laws and the elected representatives they oppose may be good or bad, but the churches insist that they along with government must be the judges of this. After 2,000 years of experience, Christian people are still considered by their leaders to be incapable of making mature political and moral decisions.

The accusation that the Catholic Church is illiberal in comparison with other churches or parties is used in the struggle for power in the south, just as it has been in the six counties. In the past all the Christian churches gained and maintained their reputation by being strict and exclusive; in recent years however public opinion changed and to be exclusive, strict or illiberal is now unacceptable. The Protestant Churches had the advantage of being presumed to be liberal while the Catholic Church had not. The reality is that both sets of churches have been exclusive and restrictive and have adopted more liberal policies in response to public opinion and in order to keep their position as acceptable leaders.

Public opinion changes and now newspapers and politicians, faced with the need to protect property, are once again emphasising the need for law, order, strict discipline and punishment. Since the churches are expected to provide stability and acceptable moral guidance, being liberal in such a climate of public opinion will probably become less popular. The power groups in politics, the media and business may then submerge their differences, form a new alliance which will include the churches in the six counties and the south to make their society more willingly illiberal. They will support and acknowledge their need for each other and the churches will remain upholders of whatever is acceptable to the power groups rather than creators of democratic change.

Although Protestant clerics were active in confrontational

politics before, during and after every major civil disturbance in the six county state and in peaceful times helped to create a culture of separateness and opposition which made civil disturbances easy to foment the churches have still been able to keep their reputation as healers and peacemakers in the six counties. But in general they look upon healing as personal repentance for having dissented and peacemaking as returning to what has been before.

When citizens formed the Civil Rights movement in the 1960s to protest against inequality, church leaders opposed them. They believed the Civil Rights movement was a threat to them and to the state. Although Catholic Church officials treated republicanism and socialism as enemies, government supporters in the six counties were told that the Catholic Church supported not only nationalism, republicanism and socialism but communism as well. Catholic Church leaders supported nationalism only to a limited degree – content with any political arrangement, even an imperial one, which would enable the church to preach its message and keep its schools – and bitterly opposed communism, socialism and republicanism. Successive Stormont administrations, politicians and preachers said the opposite and spoke of the church leaders much as they treated leaders of the republicans, socialists and communists. If the church leaders did not condemn these they were guilty themselves, if they did they were devious because they could not be believed.

Protestant Church officials wanted to keep power and influence in their own hands but were willing to allow power to politicians who declared in favour of Protestantism. The policy of their churches was to oppose socialism, republicanism and Irish nationalism, even though some of their clergy were covertly socialist, republican or Irish nationalist. The fact that republican ideals had been adopted and fostered in the six counties by Presbyterians did not make Presbyterian Church officials more favourable to them. Republicanism, socialism, Irish nationalism and Catholic power were lumped together in a package as something to be opposed even when such opposition meant a denial of history and of the Civil Rights and freedoms which church officials claimed were basic to their way of life. A Catholic republican socialist woman was probably the most formidable human enemy a six county Protestant Church official or political activist could imagine. Miriam Daly paid for it with her life. So did Máire Drumm.

In the southern state historians who divided into revisionist and anti-revisionist camps scarcely adverted to the fact that in the six counties dramatic revisions of history had occurred which affected the everyday life of the Protestant population. In more than 3,000 triumphant parades each year Presbyterians under the leadership of Presbyterian clergymen such as the Grand Master of the Orange Order Rev. Martin Smyth, celebrated with fifes, drums and banners what had been for them a disastrous defeat. The Battle of the Boyne which they joyously celebrated resulted in nearly a hundred years of persecution for their Presbyterian forebears. By a trick of revisionist history they had been persuaded to believe that it was a victory for their religious freedom. The thousands of Presbyterians who fled from the post-Boyne persecution by an Anglican inspired government had to be forgotten, the Presbyterian victims of the defeat of their revolution in 1798 had to be forgotten too. The defeat of Catholic power demanded not only an alliance of disparate Protestant groups but also that the biggest of them, the Presbyterians should falsify their own history. Catholics sometimes pointed out that whatever their Protestant fellow-citizens might think of them, at least they did not hold 3,000 marches each year to celebrate their defeats.

In the southern state because the Protestant Churches were the weaker Christian group the main power struggle was between politicians and Catholic churchmen. In the six counties the power struggle between unionist politicians and churchmen had to be discreet because of the danger of the state falling apart through fragmentation of the one party which could hold power. In the south the state would continue no matter which political faction had power – being able to change the party in power without causing the state to dissolve made it possible for southern politicians and others to engage more openly in the clergy/politician struggle. They did not do so effectively however until about the 1980s.

In the first decades the southern politicians trying to create stability in their new state had to rely on allies wherever they could be found. Churchmen were invaluable to them in reinforcing the policies of the governing party – the needs of labour, for example, had to wait and the churches blessed the politics of conservatism, possession and a military ethos. The most important thing was stability – and also unity of 'the party' – even if the cost was to be great in terms of human suffering and a rejection of principle.

On the other hand Catholic Church officials in the south, in the new circumstances and in return for their support in stabilising the state, had now a freedom and influence they never had at any other time in Irish history. With such new found freedom it is not surprising that some of them were power hungry. It is surprising that more of them did not create for themselves the Byzantine rule which bishops Browne, McQuaid and Lucey found possible, profitable and enjoyable. Those who did were experimenting with their new freedom, encouraged by a centralised Roman bureaucracy which was approaching the height of its power as controller of a universal and potentially dominant Christian Church.

The Byzantine bishops were not always wrong. What Lucey and some of his bishop colleagues said and wrote was at times a constructive critique of current politics and economics. They were not simply theocratic demagogues. Lucey's severe criticism of what he saw as the disabilities of Ireland was based upon a deep longing for development which was being frustrated by not being independent and forward looking enough. Some of it would find an echo among journalists and politicians:

> ... Take even the new factories. They are capitalist precisely as British factories are capitalist, without profit sharing, labour participation in management, distinctive technical processes or anything else to mark them off from similar factories across the Irish Sea ... they need a new spirit and new forms of organisation if they are to merit the adjective Irish on any other score than the bare fact that they are located on Irish ground, employ Irish work-

ers and are more than half owned by Irish nationals.[14]

Lucey saw the need for a new kind of industrial organisation years before the state's entry into the EEC intensified the problem of who owned the factories and what conditions were endured in them.

The power and influence of church officials in the south, irrespective of what they said or did, became more resented as the years passed and as politicians began to realise their own ability to make significant economic and political decisions, an ability never experienced in the south before and never experienced in the the six counties at all. Politicians began to contend with church officials for power over education, welfare, public policy and prestige.

At times the public assumed that in the struggles between politicians and clergy, the clergy were the winners. When a Dublin administration was driven by a combination of forces including the Catholic hierarchy and the Irish medical profession to abandon its Mother and Child scheme in 1951 this was taken as proof of the domination of government by clergy. But when the government successfully introduced a comprehensive medical scheme a short time later this was not seen as a reassurance that the politicians were winning after all. Perhaps it should have been. The dynamic of politics and public opinion could discipline even the most powerful of power groups, as Noel Browne discovered:

> My theologian had assured me that the health scheme could not be publicly condemned by even the most obscurantist bishops ... the theologian's advice to me was fully vindicated by subsequent events when the hierarchy would not dare put in writing whatever they might say individually and privately in order to frighten politicians ... the very existence of the existing free no-means-test schemes within our own social, educational and health services, as well as the British national health scheme in the north, patently gave the lie to the bishops' condemnation of the scheme.[15]

Irish people who were able to recall for nearly half a century the betrayal of Noel Browne by a Dublin administration chose not to remember that in the six counties there was a government betrayal equally worth remembering, described by Patrick Shea:

Hall-Thompson ceased to be Minister of Education in 1949 and the circumstances of his going reflected credit on no one but him. He had introduced in the House of Commons a small Bill, the purpose of which was to enable the Ministry to pay grant on the full amount of the new national insurance contributions for the teachers in those voluntary schools for which it was already bearing the full salary costs. The Second Reading in June 1949 was taken almost without comment, but when the subsequent stages came before the House some months later it was evident that some influential members of the Unionist Party had had second thoughts. Amongst the leaders of the revolt was Harry Midgley, recently converted to unionism, who made it clear that he was against making life easier for schools managed by people whose attitude to the crown and the state of Northern Ireland was less than enthusiastic. In the wheeling and dealing which followed this internal revolt Hall-Thompson (who was not an Orangeman) found it necessary to have a discussion with representatives of the Orange Order, following which he resigned from the Cabinet and accepted the lesser office of Chairman of Ways and Means. His friends thought he had been treated very shabbily.

For the rest of his life Hall-Thompson remained silent about the circumstances of his departure. I believe that if the inside story were known it would be seen to be no more creditable than the much published account of the fall of Dr Noel Browne. He, at about the same time, left the Government in Dublin after, it was said, some behind the scenes communications between the Catholic hierarchy and the Government. It could be that some of the Stormont people who cried 'shame' at the goings-on in Dublin had themselves acquiesced in a not dissimilar exercise which led to the sacrifice of a decent man within their own ranks.[16]

While the name of Noel Browne still evokes anger and letters to newspapers the names of Hall-Thompson and R. W. B. McConnell would not be recognised by many people anywhere in Ireland. Yet the fate of the two six county politicians at the hands of the clerically led Orange Order and the Presbyterian Assembly says as much about clerical domination of politics in the six counties as Noel Browne's fate does about it in the south. The problem is similar.

There is a difference however between the six counties and the south. When the postmistress of Baltinglass lost her job she got another somewhere else; when one Mother and Child scheme failed another took its place. In the six counties if discrimination took place or a project was destroyed, the job was lost and the project destroyed forever, and politicians could not hope to redress balances by becoming the governing party since there there could be no governing party except the unionists. Apart from intervention from London, which was refused as a matter of principle, such inequities were incurable. Even informal influence to get redress was limited – the nationalists in the six counties were so powerless that the only bill they succeeded in getting through the Stormont parliament was for the protection of wild birds. They could not succeed with even an amendment for the protection of their constituents whose proportion of the population was rising from one-third in the 1920s to become 43% in the 1990s.

There was an internal dynamic in the southern state which enabled some rectification of discrimination and injustice to be brought about through law and politics, in the six counties there was none; people in the south looked inward to their own institutions to demand redress, sometimes with the added impetus of international opinion. Within the six county state there was no effective dynamic to produce change and hence the people had to look outside their borders for it. Change had to be imposed by the British government because there was no dynamic strong enough to produce change within the state itself.

The Irish 1937 Constitution (Bunreacht na h-Éireann) was notable for what it did not enact as well as for what it included. De Valera resisted pressure from Continental Europe to make the Constitution that of a Catholic state. He refused to accept any church as the established state church. In Britain the question of whether to abandon the British state church was seriously discussed only when the century was drawing to a close, nearly sixty years after the Irish had decided not to allow one in the state over which they had control. But in the 1937 Constitution the state professes to accept that authority is given to government by the people while at the same time accepting the theological proposition that all power comes from God. The old doctrine of the divine right of kings is mingled with the declaration of modern democratic principle. This means that the will of the people can still be thwarted if a government, church or other body can successfully persuade citizens that the law they wish to make is not the law God wishes them to make. This, rather than the 'sectarian' nature of it, weakens the democratic power of the 1937 Constitution. Whatever laws citizens wish to make may be challenged not by God but by churches, clergy or pressure groups who can represent themselves as speaking on God's behalf. The strongest argument for removing such an article is not that it is sectarian, but that it weakens the people in their ability to make their own laws and is as unnecessary as a declaration that the people who vote are recognised as creatures of God. The 1937 Constitution encourages an untenable theology which clergy may waste time defending and which may give rise to unproductive disputes.

Even in the 1990s politicians and journalists in the six counties and the south were unwilling to risk too much by offending churchmen – they could attack easy targets, Casey, Comiskey, dead bishops, Paisley, but an imprudent attack could still lead to loss of readers and voters. As the 1990s progress this danger is receding. The increasing willingness of journalists and politicians to be openly hurtful to churchmen probably owes more to the indiscretions of the churchmen than to the courage of the others. But while easy clerical targets have been identified and personally attacked, the power structures within which they work have remained largely undisturbed because church members, politicians and journalists are unwilling to disturb them. The few church leaders who tried to dissolve the power structures of the church, Peter Birch for example and a significant number of men and women, clerical or not, were often ignored even by writers who said they were in favour of democratic change in the churches.

In the struggles for power – or to reduce power – between

politicians, churchmen and journalists the journalists were often more prominently and publicly critical of church officials than the politicians were. The politicians benefited from the chaos which churchmen created for themselves, while the most advantageous ways of benefiting from it were indicated by the journalists. By the mid-1990s anti-clerical criticism could gain readers and win votes but it still had to be selective and judicious.

Such uneasy relationships between churchmen, politicians and journalists are normal. At the end of the Second World War when General de Gaulle returned in triumph to Paris he was greeted coolly by the Catholic Church hierarchy. Yet when he was firmly in control churchmen were among the first to present themselves to him asking for control of schools. De Gaulle needed them and they needed him, so agreement between them was necessary and inevitable, in spite of their strong opposition to each other during the war. Politicians and churchmen recognise their need of each other even while engaged in their struggles for power.

Paisley led campaigns against the Catholic Church for decades. At the height of these campaigns journalists and others gave the impression that he need not be taken too seriously because he did not represent the views of the majority of decent Protestants. He represented 43% of them. From his earliest anti-Catholic crusades Paisley enjoyed support from a significant number of fellow Protestants and tacit acceptance from most of the rest. Without such support and tacit acceptance he could not have succeeded as he did. Traditionally unionists succeeded in politics according to how strongly they expressed public enmity against Catholicism. As these politicians grew older however and appeared to weaken in their opposition to their Catholic fellow citizens younger candidates challenged them. In order to survive therefore, some of these aging politicians had to pretend to anti-Catholic feelings which they no longer had. When Brookborough's political career was finished he admitted in an interview in *The Word*, a Catholic magazine, that he was really an agnostic. Brookborough had to be vehemently pro-Protestant and anti-Catholic whether he wanted to or not. He could just as readily have been an ecumenist if that had been the way to political success. Terence O'Neill recognised changing needs in the 1960s and changed his policies accordingly. So did Faulkner in the 1970s.

Brian Faulkner, the last six county prime minister, was probably not a convinced anti-Catholic but assumed the mantle of anti-Catholicism as a necessary means of making political progress. It is difficult to decide which is more immoral, the bigot who acts according to his or her anti-Catholic beliefs or the politician who is not a bigot but pretends to be one, with all the suffering for others that that entails.

The border, like religious hatred, was for some a means of providing a murky living rather than of preserving religious and political liberties. Unionists who made money from smuggling across the border disguised a love of profit by saying the border was really there to preserve political and religious liberty. Those who opened bank accounts on the southern side of the border using the Irish version of their names were not committed to keeping the border just as a means of preserving political and religious freedoms; they were committed also to preserving the Irish equivalent of a Swiss bank account.

Paisley pushed opponents aside one after another by proving that he was more anti-Catholic than they were, one of a long line of clergy politicians who did so. In politics like this the fiercest devoured the weakest of the pack. In recent times when some unionists neared the end of their political careers, they tried to win leadership not only by being more anti-Catholic than their young advancing rivals but by giving the appearance at the same time of being willing to allow Catholics some place in a society which they knew they could control only by attracting some Catholics to their side. It is a difficult strategy and most who tried it failed. Terence O'Neill failed. Brian Faulkner succeeded for a time, pretending to a bigotry he may not have had while forming an administration with Catholics in 1974, but in the end he had to retire like O'Neill to the House of Lords, overwhelmed by the support given to Paisley by 43% of Protestants who recognised him as a real anti-Catholic rather than a pretending one.

Paisley was supported by many 'lower middle class' Protestants, shopkeepers and small farmers, people of the kind who for decades had supported evangelical crusades and strongly conservative religion. He was helped also by the fear which many professional people including clergy had of him. Protestant clergy when asked to join with their Catholic fellow-citizens to curb the excesses of his campaigns would reply, 'if we oppose him many members of our congregations will leave us'.

Jesus Christ had a similar problem and solved it by telling those who wished to leave that they were free to do so.

While Paisley received the active help of tens of thousands who agreed with his campaigns he also received, and despised, the passive help of many others who did not agree with him but were too afraid or too ambitious to say so publicly.

## A LESS CLERICAL PARTY

The Social Democratic and Labour Party (SDLP) was founded in 1970 by politicians who believed the old Nationalist Party was no longer useful. For many years it had been little more than a presence in six county politics, keeping alive the idea that Ireland should be united and democratic but unable to make it so. Never able to be in government because the six counties were constructed as a one party state, unheard while abstaining from parliament and ineffective in opposition when attending, the best it could do was make deals in the corridors of Stormont with unionists decent enough to try to help but not courageous enough to do it openly. Nationalist Party meetings to select election candidates were regularly chaired by parish priests, a symbol of the influence the clergy had on them.

The founders of the SDLP wanted to change this. Some believed that a Catholic nationalist party would damage the cause of working people who needed to create co-operation among themselves and between Catholics, Protestants and others. A Catholic nationalist party which was largely business and professional middle class was unlikely to achieve this. Others believed, as Bishop Cahal Daly would say later, that 'leadership can be expected to come from the middle class' but were willing to patronise those who did not belong to it. The SDLP was a coalition of people with various interests and aims but a shared objective of achieving Civil Rights and a new deal in which they would have an important place.

All of them wanted a party which would be more than a mere presence in parliament, would act energetically and effectively to create a democratic society. They represented interests close to the old Nationalist Party, for example John Hume, and the political left, like Paddy Devlin whose election to a Belfast City Council seat in the early 1970s was opposed by senior clergy who promoted a conservative Catholic candidate of their own against him. The clerical candidate was defeated. The SDLP wanted a party without the old clerical links and so did the people.

Catholics and nationalists were thus breaking the link between clergy and political party in 1970; Protestants were discussing, without success, severing the links between their religious Orange Order and the Unionist Party in 1995, a quarter of a century later. The SDLP did not want Catholic clergy to negotiate for Catholics because they believed they were neither suitable nor competent to do it; the nationalists among them wanted to be independent politicians, the socialists among them to forge an alliance between Catholic and Protestant working people which would be impossible if politicians were too much influenced by clergy. In 1996, a quarter of a century after this break from clerical control by nationalists, unionists were represented in Westminster by 12 members of whom three, Smyth, Paisley and McCrea were Protestant clergymen.

By 1996 the socialist content of the SDLP had vanished, although the party was allied to the socialist group in the European Parliament. Paddy Devlin had left years ago and Gerry Fitt, who left the six counties, took a seat in the House of Lords, a conservative Dr Joe Hendron held West Belfast. Eddie McGrady and Seamus Mallon fitted into the pattern of traditional nationalism but with more self confidence and optimism that they could make real progress than the old nationalists ever dared to have.

The emergence of Sinn Féin with a strong challenge to the SDLP from 1983 onwards pushed the SDLP into the ambit of clergy again whether they wished it or not and the clergy into the ambit of the SDLP. The hunger-strike in which ten prisoners died was followed by a resurgence of support for Sinn Féin which alarmed the Dublin and London governments, the churches and Irish political parties including the SDLP. Although the Nationalist Party had opposed socialists and republicans more successfully than they had opposed unionists there had been no serious political rival to them or to their successors the SDLP as spokespersons for the Catholics. After the hunger-strikes however Sinn Féin was rising to challenge this position. At one period in the following years Sinn Féin got 43% of the Catholic vote.

In some places members of the SDLP and Catholic clergy began to look on each other once again as possible allies. The old identification between Nationalist Party and Catholic clergy was not revived but there was practical co-operation between them for the defeat of Sinn Féin. The SDLP had more political thrust than the old Nationalist Party and less desire to become a new clerical party but in what seemed to some nationalists a desperate situation in which Sinn Féin might become the majority leader of the Catholics, co-operation with the clergy, and also with the British government, seemed the safest thing to do. Increasing and more open co-operation between clergy and SDLP enabled both clergy and SDLP members to adopt an increasingly hostile attitude to Sinn Féin.

The alliance between John Hume and Gerry Adams in 1993, to create a new peace process, took many clergy and SDLP members by surprise. Some of them wondered what was the purpose of their being active in politics now, so important had opposition to republicans and socialists become to conservative nationalists. It seemed they hoped for an agreement with the unionists and the British government although it would take decades to achieve, but not an agreement with republicans which might be available now.

The informal alliance between clergy and SDLP could be seen more clearly in country areas throughout the six counties than in Belfast. Members of the SDLP became leading members of Catholic Church bodies, republicans usually did not. This was not because republicans were less religious than nationalists – some of them seemed more religious, more sober than some nationalists whose careless behaviour at times annoyed them – but because clergy and influential members of church congregations were more willing to welcome nationalists or conservatives into their ranks than republicans or socialists.

In Belfast the alliance could be seen at election times during the 1990s when religious sisters on their visits to the houses would gently suggest in West Belfast that, 'if you want peace you know who to vote for'. In church circles republicans and socialists were identified with disturbance and trouble, conservatives and nationalists were not. This quiet and subtly coded canvassing along with some open preaching against Sinn Féin led to a protest from a group of concerned Catholics who said they would expose church involvement in elections and campaign against it if it occurred again. Open electioneering by religious and clergy was not so observable afterwards.

Some Catholics warned that the church having broken free from attachment to one political party should never allow it to happen again. The support given to the Christian Democrats by senior churchmen in Italy and the support of Protestant clergy for religious secret societies and political parties in Ireland showed the damage alliances between clergy and political parties could do.

Eventually the question of who should negotiate for whom in the six counties seemed to be solved. By the middle of the 1990s the Catholic bishops had almost complete negotiating powers for first and second level Catholic education while the SDLP was accepted by the Dublin and London governments and churches as the negotiating body for the Catholics in other political matters. In both fields republicans or socialists were to be effectively excluded.

Neither the SDLP, the two governments nor the churches recognised that republicans had a right to negotiate for anyone, even if mandated to do so by a substantial popular vote.

Most of the politicians and church leaders believed that if negotiations could be carried on without the republicans this would be the best course. The manoeuvring of the British government following the IRA ceasefire in 1994 was designed to exclude them so as to construct a deal between the clerically influenced unionist parties, the SDLP and conservative parties in the south.

For the SDLP the most important question to be answered was whether they would have the self-confidence, or the temerity, to oppose the republicans in the expectation of making a deal with reforming unionists, or whether they would maintain the democratic unity of republican and nationalist which the Hume/Adams strategy had achieved.

# 8

# UNWELCOME PEACE

Before the IRA called its ceasefire in August 1994, British officials expressed certain 'understandings'. These were that if a ceasefire was declared the British government would be prepared to discuss every option for the future. British government withdrawal from Ireland was not excluded.

Similar 'understandings' had been expressed before. In the weekend of Bloody Sunday, January 1972, British officials including some from their ministry of defence told Irish people attending a conference near Windsor that they were willing to withdraw from Ireland. Their troops, ministry of defence officials said, were dissatisfied, some were buying themselves out. This was tolerable but, more seriously, officers were dissatisfied too, and in any case there was no cogent reason for staying. They said in effect that they were looking for a way out. On the Sunday afternoon of that weekend British paratroopers killed thirteen unarmed civilians in Derry who were peacefully demonstrating for Civil Rights.

Either the statements made during the conference by Whitehall officials were dishonest or different British power groups – civil service, home office, military – had different opinions about whether they should stay in Ireland or leave it. If the morale of the troops was as low as the ministry of defence officials said it was, letting them loose in the massacre at Derry was militarily a normal and acceptable way to raise it. It would be sufficient reason for creating the Derry massacre. The RUC was let loose on a peaceful civilian population for the same reason at Drumcree in July 1996.

Past experience would make republicans and others unwilling to believe any undertakings made orally, whether in 1972 or in 1994, by British officials. In 1994 however Irish–Americans were better informed than they were in 1972 about what was happening in Ireland and more actively involved in trying to bring about a settlement. American business people saw Ireland as an important place in which to do business. They could enter the European market through Ireland, which had an intelligent, well educated population, and labour was cheaper in Ireland than in the United States. The hastily convened Washington Conference in November 1995 on business opportunities in Ireland revealed the interests of the American business community. The late Ron Brown, secretary to the department of commerce, made the American business position clear – the Irish workforce was able, intelligent, and by American standards, cheap.

American business people wanted peace, or stability, because it would facilitate business. At the Washington Conference this was often stated the other way round, that business would bring peace. World experience had been the opposite, since more modern wars were caused by commercial expansionism, economic inequality and rivalry than by any other factor.

Bill Clinton wanted Irish–American votes for re-election. Irish Americans and others who were working consistently for democracy in Ireland because Irish people had a right to it were better informed than ever before. They were also more influential than before through years of hammering at editorial and political doors, and because of the political needs of the president and the business needs of others. American interest in Ireland for one reason or another was intense and those interested in a democracy for Ireland made their alliances accordingly. Influential business and political people in the United States became interested partners.

The British offered 'understandings', suggestions that if the republicans created a ceasefire they would respond. In view of previous experience republicans could not accept these 'understandings' without reassurances from some third party. American interest and influence could supply the reassurance they needed. Without such interest and influence the British could refuse to admit there were any understandings or concessions once the ceasefire was safely in place.

Even with the intervention of the Americans this is what they did. When the ceasefire was safely in place the 'understandings' were ignored.

Following the government's example, church leaders who had promised to help if there was a ceasefire gave no practical help after all, the RUC who had spoken of generosity stopped talking that way. The question now arising was whether American influence could be reasserted to make the British work for a democratic settlement to suit Irish people rather than a ceasefire to suit themselves.

The British government acted not according to its promises but according to its habits in its response to the ceasefire in the months that followed. They held talks with republicans while denying they were doing so, made promises of generosity while making it more and more difficult for elected representatives to have any influence on the peace process, said they would not talk to elected representatives while actually talking to them. Those who expected integrity from government were puzzled by this – it gave the impression of a government so devious that it did not know what it was doing itself. Those who did not expect integrity from government began to think ahead to what they should do to prevent a breakdown of the ceasefire or to influence the war when it started again.

When the British government acted inconsistently, or dishonestly, it was because it could not act otherwise. The British establishment is not a monolith. It consists of a number of elements, all of them powerful and struggling for more power. At times in England's history the monarchy and aristocracy were dominant, at times the state church has been influential, at other times state church or monarchy are less influential and even, as at present, threatened with extinction or marginalisation. The different elements can act in concert most of the time but there is a continuing struggle among them for supremacy – or to prevent loss of influence – by the Commons against the Lords, by the military against the civilian politicians, by the civil service against the elected representatives.

In the six counties during the 25 years' armed conflict from 1969 to 1994 the British military gained power and influence over government. They were able to influence decisions about British government policy in Ireland, to ensure by force the continuance of undemocratic rule there, to make decisions about how the Housing Executive should build its housing estates or the department of the environment its roads and streets. British army decisions affected the living conditions of Irish people and the actions of British politicians in Ireland during those 25 years. They will have a similar influence on the patterns of life in Britain in the future, if they are allowed to use the techniques of social control developed in the six counties. By the 1990s the power of the British House of Lords had long been curtailed, there was a demand for some democratisation of the monarchy, the state church had little influence on people's everyday lives and less on public life than it had some decades previously, while a struggle between prime minister and cabinet which Thatcher appeared to win, and between cabinet and Commons was continuing.

The British army whose power over decision-making had increased because its government depended upon it so much during the conflict in Ireland had to be slimmed down when the military phase of that crisis was over, not just to save money but to discipline the military who for 25 years had gained too much power within the system. Cutbacks in military spending – 152,812 military were to be reduced to 104,000 by the year 2000 – and consequent military anger followed.

There also followed the campaign for the release of Private Clegg. Clegg was put in prison for killing an Irish teenager. A campaign to set him free was supported by significant people in the British clerical and civil as well as military establishment. What was at stake was not only, perhaps not at all, the freedom of an individual soldier, or even the right of paratroopers to kill, but whether the judiciary should be able to assert authority over the military. The campaign for Clegg got unprecedented support from people who had never before been seen struggling for the rights of any prisoners, civil or military. A number of interests were involved, apart from that of righting what was seen by the campaigners as a wrong judgement. As far as possible the British army deals with its offenders internally and even when they are being processed through civil courts they are often consigned to military custody which means the military still have control rather than the civil authorities. The military are a state within the British state unwilling to allow any diminution of what they see as their rights and privileges.

In the 25 years of war in Ireland there was tension between the RUC and British military and between civil and military authorities. The military gained influence at the expense of civil and judicial authorities. In slimming down the military and slightly reducing the power they gained through their involvement in Irish affairs, the British government won. When the British army hit back and made the Clegg case a trial of strength, the army won.

The failure of the British establishment to have a coherent and integrated policy in Ireland is more easily understood when that establishment is seen as a set of elements competing for power. Some in the British foreign office may well want to leave Ireland, big business in Ireland and America would welcome stability for business, but others in influential positions do not agree with either.

The six county civil service represents and protects the interests of the British government in Ireland. It passed unchanged in outlook, ethos and recruitment procedures from the Stormont era to that of direct rule by Westminster, reinforced by officials seconded from Whitehall. Although it had engineered and worked the discriminatory and cruel Stormont system, it was commissioned to bring about change under Stormont and Westminster governments of the 1970s and to create stability in the 1990s. Their definition of peace, justice, stability, or democracy would not be the same as that of civil servants in the foreign office who from experience saw the need for occasional compromise, or of democrats within the republican tradition who demanded democratic rule because they had a right to it.

Most of these elements in British society, whether in Britain or Ireland, are pragmatic, seeking power for Britain or for their own group within Britain, but on the edges there still hovers the imperialist rear guard who refuse to believe Britain could ever be less than an imperial giant. For these, 'losing Northern Ireland' would herald the beginning of the break-up of the United Kingdom. As the 1990s went on more of them were prepared to say so. The argument was similar to that of 1916 when people of this kind believed that if they lost Ireland the empire would break up. It did.

For British and Irish loyalists the fear of opening floodgates is constant: to lose Ireland is to lose an empire; to lose Northern Ireland is to lose the United Kingdom; to lose Derry is to lose 'Ulster'; to lose the fight against Roman Catholicism is not just an event but the beginning of a deluge of evil.

For the remnant of the empire it is not a matter of discussion but inconceivable that Ireland should be independent or that other countries which had been part of the empire should be independent either. They are not capable of self-government and if they are left to themselves chaos will follow. John Major had to deal with such people hovering on the edges of the Conservative Party even at its most rational. The British Labour Party has bowed to them throughout its own pro-imperial history.[1] What they mull over in the clubs is echoed in discreet conversations among the civil servants.

Trying to strike a balance between the different pillars of its society the task for the British government in the six counties was to invent apparent changes, or even real changes, which would not threaten British control. From time to time they tried measures which would tend to make their control less oppressive, for example creating internal six county government in which Catholics would have a minor part. If such new forms of government succeeded a significant number of Catholics might accept the state – the Civil Rights movement in the 1960s demanded justice within the state not the dismantling of it. Because this seemed a useful result for the British government people were puzzled when a combination of British interests, including intelligence operators and loyalist groups, brought down the power-sharing government in 1974 which had included Catholics. But in the long term such a stable and cooperative state would possibly lead to a coalition of Catholics, Protestants and others who might come to believe their financial interests would be better served by separation from London. Stability in the short term could well be bought at the cost of breaking the union in the future.

Changes then must solve, or seem to solve, problems without creating radical changes which would have the potential of dissolving British control eventually. The problems of community relationships for example must be spectacularly addressed so as to produce stability but not in such a way as to cause a coalition between Catholics, Protestants and others whose interests did not correspond with those of the British government or its business allies. Unavoidable changes must be delayed as long as possible, granted in theory, delayed in practice or granted only with reduced effect. Granting votes for all in the early 1970s was followed by removing most of the powers of the councils for which the people were voting; funds for local industry were given only to enterprises which did not parallel or rival other businesses within the British system; fair employment laws were drafted which were bound to be ineffective.

When the British government was under severe pressure in 1969 it made the first Downing Street Declaration. Its wording was solemn and promulgating it from the steps of Number 10 Downing Street added to its solemnity. It promised changes. Many years later another Downing Street Declaration was promulgated at the same spot, promising changes. On both occasions the declarations, although they had no force in themselves but only signified intentions, were hailed as important steps forward in democratising the six county regime. The task of carrying out the reforms promised in 1969 was given over to the Stormont government, thus ensuring that they would not be put into effect.

When direct rule was imposed in 1972, again there were calls for reform and promises were made. In principle the reforms announced from London were helpful, in practice they were put into the care of the Stormont civil service which had presided over the worst excesses of the old regime and was the architect of many of them.

The pattern of British government response to cries for reform is clear. First there is denial that any reforms are needed. Then under increasing public pressure the government admits that changes are needed and will be made. Public opinion is quietened for a time but the announcement of reforms divides the community into two camps, those who know they are not enough and those who say the government should be given a chance. The process of change is given over to those who will ignore or emasculate it.

A final phase occurs when the British government, politicians, civil servants and others charged with bringing about changes finally have to do it, possibly through court action, public opinion, international pressure or, at worst, revolution. This process takes time and politicians and civil servants who have been responsible for bad practice or delayed reforms may retire, officially honoured for having done their best in such difficult circumstances. If they have done their work thoroughly they will leave behind others who will have the same attitude to change – as little as possible as late as possible since the old ways are best.

The stages in avoiding substantial change are similar in the Catholic Church. First there is denial that changes are necessary – the Latin liturgy has minor disadvantages, women are honoured not oppressed, the church needs more dedicated members rather than structural change. But time and public opinion continue to demand changes, so church officials admit that some changes are needed. But, they say, such changes, however strongly desired by them, can come about only after long preparation and discussion among officials about what the changes should be.

Changes are eventually agreed and the process of carrying out the changes is put into the hands of bishops most of whom will delay the changes or put minor changes into effect while postponing or neutralising major ones. Like ruling powers elsewhere church authorities put the achievement of change into the hands of those least likely to bring it about. Public demands are soothed and the situation remains substantially as before.

Stability in the church is reinforced by continuing to appoint officials who will conform to this pattern. In the Catholic Church the Roman authorities installed bishops who would reinforce the conservative and Roman ethos of the administration in many parts of the world and under whose guidance substantial change would be unlikely. The church bureaucracy was told that significant changes could lead to peace in the church and state but decided not to make them.

In the six counties obstacles were placed in the way of peaceful change in the state but the road was mapped wrongly as well. The primary objective was made to appear the defeat of the IRA, after which all would be well, or the achievement of 'good community relations' within the six county area, after which all would be well. Those who put forward these ideas were saying in effect, we can get peace through the defeat of the IRA or by persuading people in the streets to think better of each other. Neither of these provided a solution, because the reasons for the conflict were deeper and older than the IRA or the varying, shifting crowds opposing each other in the streets or on the football terraces. The conflict stemmed from the British government's desire for military bases and control of the Irish economy and could not be reduced to easier terms.

If the people are at fault because they cannot live peacefully together, then before they can be given effective political structures they need to be taught to live at peace. This was suggested by, among others, John Hume who had probably more experience of how other people govern themselves than any other Irish politician. The contrary argument is that neither the Irish nor any other people can afford to wait until they love each other before building political structures which suit them. It was not done in Ireland in the 1920s, structures were imposed upon people who were still at war. It was not done in Switzerland, the United States, Belgium, Newfoundland; people were not required to wait until everyone was at peace before creating political structures which suited them – they created political structures which took account of the needs, genius and antagonisms of the people and which arose out of them.

The Irish were told, and many of them unwisely believed, that they, unlike other peoples, could not set up political structures until they were reconciled to each other. Those who made this suggestion had no plans for dissolving the power of the institutions, secret like the Orange Order or public like the churches and other political interest groups, which kept them apart no matter how well they tried to integrate. Attempts to live peacefully together while these associations were not restrained by adequate political structures and laws could go on forever and be frustrated forever. Living peacefully together depended upon having adequate structures and laws, so if the creation of such structures and laws is delayed, peaceful living is impossible. In this as in so many other things the Irish were treated as oddities, sometimes by each other.

The doctrine of 'No Structures Without Reconciliation' suited those who wanted to make no change at all, to delay change, or make minimal change. As long as it was accepted, political change could be prevented by creating another round of community conflict; a religious march here, a killing there, burning an Orange hall, breaking the windows of a Catholic church and the politicians and preachers who did not want change could say, clearly we are not ready for political change yet. The counter argument was that the breaking and killing can stop only when adequate political structures are in place which will dissolve the power of secret societies and within which people are adequately defended and can make real decisions about their lives.

In Belgium one of the world's most famous universities Louvain/Leuven had to be divided as part of a new political arrangement. The Belgians did not say, they could not afford to say, let us wait until we are all at peace before creating suitable political structures. They knew they might wait forever. In Ireland the same mentality which said, we cannot share Christ in the Eucharist until we all believe the same things, said, we cannot share government, power, and prosperity until we all think alike. Even those Christians who said they needed a firm framework of law and order to enable them to behave lovingly towards each other refused to discuss the creation of a fresh political framework to enable all the people to live and work in harmony. They demanded an impossible reconciliation among them first.

Irish people were persuaded to believe they were unique – they could not fight for their freedom, they must not decide freely who their elected representatives will be, they must be at peace with their neighbours before being allowed to create political structures, they cannot wage war, they can only cause troubles, they are the only people in the democratised world forbidden to talk about defeating their political opponents, even those who persecuted them, having to be reconciled to them instead. These myths prevented realistic political discussion and were created and kept alive by those who did not want change.

None of the powerful groups could or would dissolve themselves. They could be dissolved through discussion among the people as a whole, however, because discussion could lead to a popular demand for democratically shared power and responsibilities. Such discussion had to be inhibited by promises or threats, sometimes by assassination. Loyalists such as Sammy Smyth and John McKeague, and members of the loyalist 'left' discussed but did not survive.

When changes could no longer be avoided power struggles went on even among those who wanted them. Some politicians and church officials seemed to prefer no change to change engineered by someone else. The official Catholic Church attitude to Civil Rights was that changes should be made in the six county state giving Catholics a fair deal, but this fair deal should be negotiated between church officials and the government. Churchmen should be assisted, not directed, by friendly politicians. If others, republican, socialist or nationalist, tried to create a better situation for Catholics many churchmen would view them with suspicion and perhaps oppose them even though their Civil Rights aims were broadly the same. They believed they had the right and the ability to make government respond for the right reasons and implied that anyone else trying to influence government would be doing so for suspect reasons.

The apparent success of southern Catholic bishops in influencing governments in Dublin may have encouraged six county bishops to believe they could influence the Stormont or British governments similarly. The success of the southern bishops however was illusory because by the 1990s the bishops in the south had been defeated on almost every issue and control of education was moving slowly away from the strong clerical control of the past.

Senior members of the clergy in Ireland seemed to believe that politicians chosen by the people did not have the same authority as clergymen appointed by the pope. Senior six county clergy saw the increasing influence of elected people in the south and abroad, and yet at home in the six counties believed they could afford to keep power or influence from such people. The affair of the Mater Infirmorum Hospital in Belfast illustrated this.

In 1972 the hospital became part of the British state system. It had become too expensive to run as a private or church institution. The Stormont government had resisted all pleas to subsidise it fully or help it financially in a realistic way. As costs rose it became only a matter of time until a decision had to be made that the unionist regime would either subsidise the hospital adequately or take it over.

Campaigns to get money for the hospital had gone on for decades, in which the church hierarchy who controlled the hospital were helped by friendly nationalist and Labour politicians at Stormont. These often had to plead for the hospital without adequate information being given to them by the hospital's governors. When asking the government to negotiate with church officials they admitted that they had not been given enough information to enable them to negotiate effectively themselves.

The church officials believed that here, as in the case of civil rights and schools, improvements could be brought about through interaction between churchmen and government, assisted by friendly politicians who might persuade the Stormont government to listen to them. There was never any question of the church officials asking politicians to negotiate directly with government for schools, hospital or civil rights with the churchmen assisting them.

The policy of being the negotiators for the Catholics while holding politicians and other possible professional negotiators at arm's length can be seen also in the six county Catholic bishops' protests against discrimination and in their manoeuvring for negotiating positions in 1969 and afterwards. The warning by Bishop Philbin during the Civil Rights movement, 'Don't be led by the Reds' seems bizarre now in view of the fact that the leaders of the Civil Rights movement were conservative and largely middle class with little possibility of a take-over of the movement by any radical group. Philbin's warning had more to do with a church policy of being the sole negotiators for Catholics than with any real threat from 'reds' or anyone else.

This policy was a source of weakness. When the Nationalist Party dissolved in the early 1970s the SDLP which replaced it was determined not to become another clerical party. Privately they gave assurances that it would not. During and after the hunger-strikes in the 1980s the SDLP came strongly within clerical influence and senior church officials looked to it as a party through which they could directly influence politics again. Some Catholics warned that having got rid of the connection between the Nationalist Party and the clergy Catholics should not recreate an alliance with any political party for any reason. The close connection of Protestant clergy with political parties in the six counties had damaged both clergy and politics – their political parties lost independence, churches lost their followers – and there was also the example of the Christian Democrats in Italy, supported by the Vatican and turning out to be among the corrupt political parties in Europe. Church leaders in Ireland chose to foster an alliance between themselves and the British government and left the political representatives chosen by the Catholic vote still on the margins.

Nationalist politicians in the six counties had a similar attitude – they would work to democratise the regime but believed change should happen through interaction between themselves and government. Any initiative by people outside their party was unwelcome and should be opposed. The Catholic churchmen believed they should control change and therefore marginalised the nationalist politicians; nationalist politicians believed they should control change and therefore marginalised republicans and others. The opposition of both to the MacBride and other campaigns is more easily understood in the light of this.

As I said earlier it may be difficult to understand why church officials or democratic politicians opposed the campaign in the United States for adoption of the MacBride Principles for fair employment or the boycott against Bushmills Whiskey. Both campaigns were directed in a peaceful way against anti-Catholic discrimination in the six counties. The Mac-Bride Principles were accepted by a large number of American States and city councils and enshrined in law, Bushmills employees were overwhelmingly Protestant. But for the official Catholic Church and the SDLP political change had to come about through them and not through campaigns run by others whose campaigns they did not direct and over whose actions they had no control.

Some church and political representatives suggested that these anti-discrimination campaigns were fronts for Sinn Féin or the IRA and that they had little real regard for Civil Rights except as a weapon against the British government. The same had been said about the Civil Rights movement in the 1960s, that the campaigners were really looking not for Civil Rights but for the subversion of the state. But whereas the churches and conservative politicians had discouraged or disregarded the Civil Rights movement in Ireland they actively opposed the MacBride and other private citizens' campaigns abroad. Members of Catholic religious orders including the Jesuits, Catholic organisations including the Knights of St Columbanus and Catholic clergy including members of the hierarchy went to the United States to join in the British challenge to the MacBride Principles for Fair Employment. The Church of Ireland and the Presbyterian Church created their own opposition to MacBride.

One of the major difficulties in creating a united effort for justice among democrats is such reluctance of political and other groups to support efforts which are not begun or controlled by them. This was recognised by John Hume and Gerry Adams when they joined in creating an initiative for peace which led to the IRA ceasefire of 1994. Those within the SDLP who opposed this alliance were not thereby rejecting peace but were refusing to recognise that peace should ever be brought about by republicans. It would be unfair to say that politicians or churchmen in general prefer no change at all to change wrought by someone else; they believe they can create peace and a new deal without the republicans, provided they are given the freedom and the time to do it.

Republicans do not agree. They believe that unless political opposition to injustice and for political change is united, the only effective action left is a military one – nationalists or republicans separately do not have the diplomatic influence or political power to force change on a British government unwilling to grant it. For republicans the choice is either to create a united political front or to see a renewed military struggle whether they want it or not.

The subtlety of their position or the dangers of not appreciating it are not always understood. Conservative nationalists argue that the first task is to defeat the republicans, co-operating with the Dublin and London governments to do it if necessary, and a new social order will follow. They do not accept that if the two governments succeeded in destroying the republicans who have represented 43% of the Catholic electors, the SDLP's negotiating power would be significantly weakened.

For politicians and church leaders who said publicly that a new social order must involve acceptance of all political and religious ideals, the decision that they must defeat the republicans as a first step towards peace was an extraordinary one.

Just as extraordinary was the determination and courage of John Hume and Gerry Adams who recognised that party prestige must be only of secondary importance in a shared pursuit of justice.

# 9
# AFTER THE WAR WAS OVER

After the republican and loyalist ceasefires in 1994, old rivalries between religious groups began to re-appear in the six counties. During the 25 years of conflict leaders of the churches had an informal alliance against the republican movement. The ceasefires weakened this alliance.

In September 1995 a Church of Ireland rector in Belfast, Rev. William Hoey, a member of the Orange Order, attacked Cardinal Cahal Daly in his parish newsletter, describing him as 'a red-hatted weasel'. The cardinal had shown exceptional friendship to Protestants and often urged Catholics to understand their view and reach out in friendship to them. No Catholic Church leader in Ireland had insisted so frequently on friendship between religious groups.

This policy made him a greater problem for some Protestant clergy than if he had been indifferent or hostile to them. If Catholic clergy adversely criticised them they knew where they stood, in opposition. If a Catholic clergyman was friendly, one had either to accept the friendship or condemn him as a hypocrite trying to seduce the unwary. The Rev. Hoey chose the second of these, and chose the symbol of animal treachery to do it.

It would have been impolitic to say such a thing when Church of Ireland and Roman Catholic leadership were united against the IRA. When the IRA declared a ceasefire – and the British government was showing they believed the war was over by dismantling perimeter fencing around their military barracks – the need for political solidarity among some church officials seemed to be over too. Christians could once again show animosity towards fellow Christians and others. Some had never given it up, some never had it and some had hidden it for the sake of solidarity against the IRA.

The Hoey outburst represented the views of a significant number of clergymen whose religious animosities hidden for political reasons during the war were likely to erupt again once the war appeared to be over. The Anglican archbishop of Armagh, Robin Eames, regretted that 'the words had been used', said that 'everyone is entitled to personal opinions', that what was said 'did not represent the views of the Church of Ireland' and that 'he regretted the use of these words about someone with whom he worked very closely'.

The statement lacked any expression of personal regard for Daly. Having expressed regret for the words used, he did not make clear whether if opposition and distrust had been expressed in less offensive terms they might have passed without comment. His rebuke to Hoey was minimal, a message to other clergy equally antagonistic that Eames was not prepared to defend Daly or seriously oppose any of his clergy who might attack him or other members of the Roman Catholic Church. The alliance between Catholic and Anglican churchmen put together during the war was not necessarily forever.

On the day Hoey's attack was quoted in the newspapers public opinion polls revealed that most Protestants believed the RUC were doing a good job. During the previous month the RUC had batoned Catholic protesters so severely that a senior policeman found it necessary to express regret publicly for it. The public opinion poll suggested that most Protestants were more in favour of what the RUC had done than were the senior RUC members themselves.

People in the six counties were now facing a situation similar to that in European countries after the Second World War. Before the war Christians in Holland for example, were divided, had separate schools, separate publications, broadcasting stations, churches and associations. During the war they were forced to work together and many found themselves fighting, being imprisoned, dying together, Jews, Catholics, Protestants, Socialists, Communists and others.[1]

By the end of the war many people had come to believe that their divisions had been unnatural and unnecessary and they should get rid of them. Christians were unsure. Some welcomed the opportunity to get rid of unnecessary division and make a fresh, united start to create a new social and religious life. Others believed the old divisions should be renewed and revitalised.

> The ideals (of a new unity) proved illusory. The progressive young Catholics remained small in number, while the conservative minded remained just as numerous as before. This latter group immediately set to work on restoring the pre-war situation, openly encouraged by the bishops; they brought back the Catholic political party, Catholic organisations and clubs, the solid principles of our ancestors, etc. All was of course to be modernised and adjusted to the new age, but the hour of a breakthrough towards a new set-up had not yet come. As before it was a matter of 'prudent government', 'really solid discussion', 'we must proceed step by step' and so on ... (but) the isolation policy is gone now ... Social relations have not suffered in any way and the various groups of the population have learned to appreciate one another, which has made for better co-operation.[2]

While Christian factions in Holland argued the people as a whole went the way of post-war Europe and became less concerned with whether the Christians united or not, preferring to be left alone and free from involvement in wasteful Christian quarrels.

With the 25 year armed conflict over in the six counties the problem was smaller but similar. Would church leaders, united in a war effort against what they saw as a common enemy, the republican movement, and in criticism of the loyalist armed campaigns, now revert to their old rivalries? Or would they try to create unity and integration among Christians and between Christians and the community as a whole?

For some the only Christian way forward was to renew religious controversy and try to get converts from within what they saw as other Christians' territory. The Methodists announced a new evangelising campaign targeting North and West Belfast, areas with significant and increasing Catholic populations. Irish Christian Assemblies in Limerick sent pamphlets to Catholics in Belfast slowly recovering from the trauma of 25 years of war posing the question: 'When a Roman Catholic

Gets Saved, Should He Leave His Church?' and offering help if he desired to do so.

For others, unity and respect among Christians themselves and between Christians and others were necessary for their own sake as well as to avoid further conflict. Others shared the opinion of Bernadette McAliskey, that whether the churches change their ways or not is a matter of indifference:

> Now I look around at all the problems we have, and I have come to a position that the church is no problem to me, no problem at all. I don't go. I don't pay, I don't listen to that church ... the world will progress, humanity will win out, that is our belief ... if through the base groups the church survives, then it will be part of that movement. If the church doesn't survive I don't care. I have actually come to that point and I think that maybe the church in its officialdom doesn't realise how many people have. As somebody who remembers, not indeed fondly, but who attributes, and is not ashamed to attribute, a great depth of what I am to being born and raised in the Catholic Church of my mother and father, I don't care if the church survives or not.[3]

The Christians who wanted to keep and revitalise differences found their task easier by the fact that during the 25 years of armed conflict churches and church organisations did not change their official opposition to sharing marriage, worship, buildings, places of residence and work, wealth, ideas or political power.

The refusal of Christians to allow fellow Christians of different traditions to share their Eucharist was a powerful symbol of their unwillingness to share anything else. In 1996 Tony Blair sharing the Eucharist together with his Roman Catholic wife was the subject of an significant controversy which showed that for many Christians purity of exclusive doctrine was still more important than love strong enough to share Christ. For them the world should go on suffering its anger and hurt rather than be relieved a little by a fresh interpretation of Christian beliefs.

Inter-church meetings of officials were unlikely to be more effective in creating inter-Christian peace after the war than attempts to create an effective ecumenical movement had been before it. Those taking part in inter-church meetings, academics, church officials, etc., might come a little closer to each other, but since their meetings were not fully inclusive of all Christians they might well drive others away.

Among the Protestant Church based organisations the Orange Order became more publicly active although its influence was weakening and could be weakened further by the enactment of effective fair employment laws. The existing laws even up to the late 1990s were defective but the campaigns which forced the government to make them – the MacBride campaign abroad, boycott at home and public education everywhere – helped to strengthen public opinion against discrimination. Clergy and politicians who controlled the Orange Order saw that the power of the secret societies would be weakened if fair employment laws were effective. It was for this reason that they opposed campaigns and effective laws for fair employment – as more and more people brought cases of unfair employment to tribunals, it was becoming more expensive to discriminate and the power of the religious secret societies to determine who would get jobs was lessened. As their job patronage lessened the membership and power of the religious secret societies would lessen also; many Protestant men would see little point in joining a lodge if it was no longer able to get them jobs.

While the power of the religious secret societies was weakening as more people brought cases to tribunals, this was not fast enough to ensure rapid changes. Firms like Ford and Universities such as Queen's in Belfast had to pay out tens of thousands of pounds in legal costs and compensation for what they had done but those discriminated against were still without the jobs they were entitled to and since the money came out of the public purse individuals in commercial and academic institutions could still discriminate without any penalty to themselves. The British government was unwilling to take the next logical step of demanding that jobs should be given to those who deserved them and that compensation and legal costs for economic cruelty should come from the pockets of those who caused it, not from those of the general public, many of whom knew nothing about it.

In the summer of 1996 the Orange Order's insistence on forcing parades through Catholic areas and confronting the police in a show of strength had more to do with the declining membership and influence of the Order and the desire of some militant members to replace its ageing leadership, reasserting control of politics, than it had with pure bigotry of members. The strength which the Order was losing through waning ability to arrange jobs was to be renewed through an appeal to primitive religious fears. There was a struggle for power between the leadership of the Order and that of the RUC, between those in the Order who wanted to take control of it and the ageing leadership who had it. The events at Drumcree clarified some of these issues. They also enabled a few members of the Presbyterian and Church of Ireland communities to voice their concern that their churches were being used in such political struggles.

Canon William Arlow and Dean Victor Griffin expressed the ideas of such people in the Church of Ireland and a statement issued by a group of Presbyterians spoke for some members of their church, no one could estimate how many in either case:

> The widespread perception of Protestantism (closely allied to the Orange Order) as primarily the religious dimension of unionism and unionism as exclusively Protestant was vividly reinforced by pictures on the TV of Drumcree parish church amidst a sea of Union flags and Orange banners ...[4]

Canon Arlow deplored the silence of Protestant Church leadership when the church was being used for political purposes.

The Presbyterian group expressed similar disquiet:

> We wish to confess with deep anguish the sins of disobedience, rebellion, anger and sectarianism which were perpetrated on the whole community in the supposed cause of civil and religious liberty ... those who vociferously claim to represent the Protestant community do not represent the authentic voice of Presbyterianism.[5]

Interpreting incidents like those of the summer of 1996 when repeated attempts were made to force, and to resist, politico/ religious processions through Catholic areas as motivated only by blind bigotry hinders a realistic analysis of what is happening in the six counties, and why. There are economic and political reasons why it is done and there are people within the churches who recognise that this is so. Their protests at the use of religion for politics, however, came too late to prevent the worst effects of it.

Church leaders during and after the war preached unity and tolerance but continued to inhibit people from integrating in ways that were natural to them – through education, shared housing, shared jobs, inter-marriage. Twenty-five years of war had not changed official church attitudes very much. The lone voice of Michael Hurley, SJ, in the 1960s asking people not only to tolerate but to welcome inter-church marriages had long been forgotten. The British government's arrangements for Catholic hierarchical control of Catholic schools while gradually eroding the Protestant clerical control of the state sector gave cause for further divisions and rivalries.

In 1995 when the ceasefires were about nine months old the irritation of Protestant Church leaders at this situation appeared in public. The Church of Ireland made two submissions to the Forum for Peace and Reconciliation in Dublin. The first was bland with little more than pious wishes for the future. The second was more demanding. It showed the resentment of Church of Ireland leaders against what the British government had done in education since direct rule began in 1972. They asked that there should be no further lessening of Protestant Church influence on education boards. The lessening of Protestant clerical control of state schools had been significant.

During the 1980s some of the functions of the education boards relating to Catholic schools were given over to the CCMS, the Council for Catholic Maintained Schools. The council consists of the six county bishops and their appointees. The Church of Ireland submission said that an independent body similar to the CCMS should be set up to look after the interests of the Protestant Churches in education.

In the six county education system there are independent Protestant and Catholic schools, state schools, some integrated schools including Irish language schools. The education of most Catholics at primary and secondary level is governed by the CCMS. The council came into being gradually and almost by stealth, taking over many of the functions of the state appointed education boards. Protestant Church leaders believed this system increased Catholic power and hence their submission to the Forum saying that another council on similar lines should be set up for them. Such a council with functions similar to those of the CCMS would further dilute the power of the government's education boards and enhance that of church officials in general without diluting the power of the Catholic bishops. No one made the suggestion that, on the contrary, the CCMS should be dissolved and the education system should cease to be either controlled or necessarily influenced by clergy of any church. The churches were not prepared for this, although some clerics would have welcomed being relieved of the work of educational administration they were no longer sure was specifically theirs. Clerical control of schools did not keep people coming into church to hear clergy preach. The opposite might well be happening. The advantages of clergy controlling education may well have been exaggerated. The Church of Ireland submission to the Forum for Peace and Reconciliation showed that attitudes about control of education had not changed among church officials after the 25 years of war.

The six county state in 1996 was governed by Patrick Mayhew who in turn was governed by the Northern Ireland civil service; the Catholic Church was headed by Cardinal Cahal Daly, a kindly conservative in religion and politics; Archbishop Robin Eames presided over the Church of Ireland having crowned his career by joining the House of Lords, described in one editorial as 'probably the most undemocratic body in the European Union'. In my view there was little possibility of rekindling a reforming fire from any ashes of Christian idealism still smouldering in Stormont or Armagh and a great possibility that any reforming fire among the people would be quenched by the establishment and hierarchy.

Church officials were living in separate worlds even from church people in general, with separate ideals, aims and methods, neither communicating sufficiently to accept ideas from the other. In 1994 at the end of the military campaigns when there was cautious talk of change in the state and the church, the three bishops in the six county diocese of Down and Connor, Ireland's second largest, were distinguished, one in mathematics, one in ancient classics, the third in social sciences. All three were conservative and had strong Roman connections. It was a symbol of a pattern now established of appointing Catholic bishops in Ireland from among conservative academics with strong Roman connections. One of the results of this policy was episcopal pronouncements achieving cohesion through blandness.

Rifts began to appear however when people became more aware of how deep the crisis within the Irish churches was and how powerful, well off, but irrelevant the churches had become. Cardinal Daly, conservative member of the Roman Curia, the central ruling body of his church, was more openly and frequently criticised by people who wanted to see changes in Catholic Church policy. The criticisms of the 1960s were concerned largely with liturgy and financial accountability, those of the 1990s with the church's politics as well; by the 1990s most of those who had campaigned for reform of church liturgy, doctrine or laws had settled for absence of conflict and a limited amount of change. Discussion of liturgical formulas seemed unimportant now when discussion was raging about whether the churches supported oppression or condoned revolution and whether it was even worthwhile to have churches at all. The eye of the storm had shifted from the comfortable middle class faithful who could worry about the position of their altars to those mainly working class and poor members who worried about whether the churches would save their homes from burning or their children from being murdered.

Some bishops wanted substantial change in church policies. Brendan Comiskey, Bishop of Ferns, said clerical celibacy should be discussed and Cardinal Daly sharply and publicly replied that it should not, and that a bishop's private opinions had no authoritative value. Clearly there could be differences between what even an Irish bishop believed and what the Roman Curia taught. It had long become clear that there were significant differences between what the Roman Curia taught and what the people believed. The cardinal as a member of the Roman Curia took the official and authoritative line, Bishop Comiskey disagreed with the official line and it seemed that other disagreements among other bishops might follow. The Romans, however, had ensured that their directives would be followed by appointing bishops who were academics, and therefore professionally remote from everyday affairs, and had a strong attachment to Rome, even if the general public whom they were appointed to serve, knew little about them.

Seán Brady, appointed coadjutor to Cardinal Daly was virtually unknown to the public before his appointment, having spent many years in Rome and only a few in parochial work in Ireland. Philip Boyce appointed in 1995 to Raphoe, a diocese in the north-west of Ireland had spent the 30 years previous to his appointment working in Rome. In this, as in other appointments, the academic qualities and the Roman connection were clear, the pastoral connection with the diocese to which the appointment was made was not.

One consequence of this Roman policy is that even if church leaders privately or publicly assent to the need for change, they will implement it only hesitantly if at all. A succession of similar appointees can bring change to a halt and even restore things to where they were before. As long as the power to appoint Catholic bishops is centralised in Rome this will continue and even if creative changes are made locally through the insistence of some bishops they cannot have any assured permanency. In this as in many issues affecting the Catholic Church the decentralising of the church is a key to solving problems.

The six counties are politically and economically under the control of London and cannot develop according to their needs and abilities. Catholics are further inhibited in their cultural, religious and social development by the Roman Church bureaucracy. For all the people living in the six counties intellectual and spiritual development is hindered by the prevailing public ethos which is one of threat, fear, laziness and fatalism.

If they are to develop economically, politically, socially and religiously, they must shake themselves free from all the undemocratic restraints which have their roots not in Ireland but in London, Rome and Geneva. Beside these, the restraints imposed by Brussels seem relatively superficial and bearable.

# 10

# FAITH WORTH THE PRICE

At the Second Vatican Council (1962–65) Catholic bishops tried to recover the authority and position they had lost to the Curia, the Roman bureaucracy which had succeeded in centralising decisions in the Catholic Church to the point of inertia. They won a paper victory, as the council produced documents which could have helped the Catholic Church to become once again a living body rather than a law-bound institution. It produced nothing that had not been suggested and developed by writers in Continental Europe for some years past. Instead it carefully selected what was acceptable in contemporary religious thinking and what was not. Although the council could have enlivened the church, the dynamic of it was to limit and control the current of theological speculation and creativeness which had occurred especially since the Second World War. Like any other church council it became also the site for a struggle for power in which many bishops and others appealed for local autonomy while the Curia worked for the continuation of centralised government.

When the council was over and the bishops dispersed the Curia reasserted itself, appointing bishops with strong Roman connections, sometimes without adequate, or any, consultation with other bishops, clergy or members of local churches.

When Bishop Brendan Comiskey mildly challenged the increasing influence of the Curia in 1994 he was voicing not only his own opinion about current church issues but also the discontent of some bishops and others who were convinced that the centralising Roman bureaucracy of the Catholic Church must be curbed if the Catholic Church were not to sink further into materialism and ineptitude. The materialism and ineptitude could be addressed only by leaders of spiritual and intellectual quality who recognised real issues in their dioceses and in the church and understood how to deal with them. The centralising Roman establishment was materialistic, expensive and inefficient.

Bishop Comiskey did not get time to expand on what should be done in the church because he was soon embroiled in controversy about his own private life. The press, with whom he had had good relations and which in theory advocated greater freedom and reform in the churches, successfully diverted public discussion away from the issues he raised and on to his personal life. The issues he raised, celibacy and openness in discussion, were aspects of church life which needed to be raised and whether Bishop Comiskey survived or not they were certain to be raised again sooner or later. Whoever raised them however would have to contend with the same negative press reaction as Bishop Comiskey had experienced. The press was willing not only to discuss his private life but to ensure that in doing so it would bury from sight all the issues of reform which he raised.

Within a few months another Irish bishop, Willie Walsh of Killaloe raised the question of compulsory celibacy again. This time the press could not divert the discussion away from the issues and on to the private life of this bishop who was less vulnerable than Comiskey. Sooner or later the tactic of diverting discussion away from central issues and on to the credentials of those who raised them must stop working. The tactic is used with almost invariable success as those who raise significant issues in church and state are forced to discuss their sexual or political preferences instead.

Church leaders, politicians and the press inhibit discussion about important issues by finding a diversionary topic or inventing one to engage public attention. The diversionary topic may be important or not. What is important is that what is discussed should be decided not by the people at large but by the power groups, press, church officials, business people, politicians and others.

It was Voltaire who said, 'When bishops have nothing to say about God they take to moralising'. The emergence of the IRA in the early 1970s gave church leaders an opportunity for moralising. They could condemn the IRA in frequent statements and this was all the public came to expect from them. By doing so they demonstrated their respectability in supporting law, order and government. They did not contribute effectively to changing the war into peace. During the 25 years of war they made no statements of significant theological value about the existence of God, the origin and meaning of life or other vital questions to which people wanted answers. Most of the ideas for social change came from other people and often from other countries.

When people moved away from churches it was not because their leaders did not speak out but because they did not speak out about the right things. Basic questions were not answered. Sex, law and order dominated their statements. Sons and daughters asked for bread and were given pamphlets about condoms.

Those who moved away from churches, the leaders said, did so because they were becoming more materialistic. One of them said about young people that their attitude was due 'to their adopting the ideas of Thatcherite consumerism'. They did not accept that church leadership might be inadequate or official church teaching ill-fitting with modern needs and potential. While it was admitted that mistakes had been made, these were said to be temporary mistakes but not serious flaws.

It could be argued on the contrary that the churches did not measure up to the idealism of a people who were willing to believe what the churches taught provided it was reasonable and relevant to believe it. While they issued no significant statements about fundamental questions church leaders seemed to take for granted that God exists, that no proof for their teaching was needed and people should believe it on their authority. They did not cater for those who doubted or disbelieved, or for those who wanted religiously satisfying and intellectually convincing reasons for believing what they taught. Leaders and preachers seemed to think they need do no more than tell people they had a duty to believe – churchmen did not have to give them convincing reasons for believing. Penalties for not believing were announced with authority, reasons for believing seldom mentioned.

When the 25 year armed conflict ended with the IRA's ceasefire in 1994 the churches' appeal to people to take religion seriously as a help to peace was based increasingly on accepting Jesus Christ at a personal and often emotional level rather than as the proposer of a useful philosophy of life. This was reflected in religious broadcasting which relied increasingly on an emotional appeal to rely on Jesus to solve difficulties without discussion of the intellectual and spiritual power which Christians used to claim God had given them to solve problems themselves. Christians who had observed during 25 difficult years that prayer was often not answered, found it increasingly unlikely that they could solve their problems by laying them on the shoulders of the Lord Jesus as preachers bade them to.

More Catholics in the six counties, politically aware of themselves and their dignity, required reasons for what they were asked to do or believe. Being instructed to believe was not enough. For decades they and their fathers and mothers, grandfathers and grandmothers had been persecuted because they were Catholics, refused jobs and driven out of their homes in regular state-provoked pogroms. They were derided because they were Catholics. They were told by parents and preachers that this was the price they had to pay for their faith. Young people of the 1990s wanted to know what Catholicism offered that was worth the high price they had to pay for it, and why they should remain Catholic if they considered the price too high. Religion had been used for centuries to divide and conquer people in a continuing struggle for power in Ireland. They and their forebears were often pawns in a cynical game. What compelling reason was there to cling to a way of life or a set of beliefs if this meant perpetual disadvantage? To do it for oneself might be reasonable but to insist that one's children do it also was to risk committing an injustice against them.

The questions asked by young and old especially during the past three decades in the six counties were not the academic posers of a religious knowledge class but questions of life and death, of having a meaning for one's life or not. It often seemed to the questioners that they would have to look for answers outside the churches and from people other than religious leaders. Groups formed among the people who went their own Christian way, discontented with inadequate answers, disdainful when they got no answers at all. Criticism of the churches became more open and impatient and those who wanted to get rid of what was wrong and recreate what was right went their own way more and more openly, inviting church leaders to come with them but no longer inhibited if they did not.

Some insisted on open discussion and organised independent conferences for it without waiting for church synods. Others campaigned for equality for all church members including ordination for women. Others explored the meaning and experience of Christians in Ireland before the imposition of Roman customs and law. Some worshipped and celebrated the Eucharist with a simplicity which recalled the gatherings of the earliest Christians around their Agape table. Men and women who had left formal ministry in the church explored ways to minister again using their experience and gifts for the benefit of their fellow citizens whether the church authorities approved of them doing it or not.

In both church and state the challenge was not to authority, it was to those who claimed it to prove they had it or else to step aside and allow people to find the roots of real civil and religious authority for themselves.

# 11

# DEMOCRACY DENIED

Democracy is not generally accepted in Ireland. What is accepted is a form of government capable of developing into democracy but not yet developed far beyond the model accepted in the 1920s. It is assumed that the structures of government in Ireland and Britain need no further development – more suitable people could be elected but basically the system is a democratic one which needs no fundamental development or change.

In an RTE television programme in 1980 it was suggested that democratic institutions as we know them in Ireland could be developed so that, for example, all governments in the future would be coalitions not of two or three parties but of all parties, creating in effect a system of government which maximises the democratic voting power of the electors.

No elector votes on polling day to put his or her party into opposition. Electors vote to place their party in government. Respecting this decision must mean eventually a coalition of all parties, possibly with independents coalescing to obtain seats in proportion to the number of votes for them. This could be seen as the next inevitable logical step forward for democracies and one which is inevitable in the six counties if it is to remain a separate political unit. Garret Fitzgerald who took part in the discussion rejected this, reflecting the view of many people who cannot see any system of parliamentary government except that of the confrontational party system. One party wins, even, as in Britain, with a minority of the votes cast, and the rest have to go into opposition. This is our system and they believe no other need be envisaged.

But on the other hand, when new forms of government have to be devised for Ireland, it would be possible to create structures there which would represent a more advanced democratic government than that available in any other country. The question is not whether this can be done but whether governments and politicians will take the opportunity to do it.

The ideas expressed by loyalists and working class union-ists in the 1970s were ignored by those who could have en-couraged both the ideas and those who put them forward. Those who refused to discuss them must bear some of the re-sponsibility for the emergence of the killing campaigns which followed. A quarter of a century later journalists are writing about 'cantonisation 'on the Swiss model as if it was a newly emerging idea. It had been discussed in the early 1970s while repartition was being discussed and rejected at the same time. Repartition, it was believed even then, would create not a coalition of free people in Ireland but a reservation for Pro-testants in the north-east. Mature people with ideas for dis-cussions at that time were ignored. The failure to discuss solu-tions in the north-east was due not to lack of ideas but to refusal of journalists, politicians, clergy, academics and others to dis-cuss what people were suggesting. As intellectual inertia was prevalent among themselves, inertia was the fashion and must be maintained even if it cost lives.

Democracy is not static. It has to develop, otherwise it be-comes an atrophied system in which people are governed by rules laid down by a majority so defined as not to represent most of the people most of the time. A more shocking des-cription of the system is that present forms of democratic rule in Britain and Ireland are designed to exclude large sections of the population, as much as half, from government for periods of four or five years at a time.

Such a system is acceptable to most Irish and British people. Although the unionist system in the six counties was specially designed to exclude Catholics permanently, politicians and church leaders still feel able to talk about a 'return to demo-cracy' as if the Stormont system had satisfied them. The demo-cratic system as we know it even at its best prevents people from taking significant control of their own affairs or experimenting with new forms of government suited to their own needs, potential and history.

Logical changes in our institutions and structures of government may have to wait until we are forced to rebuild after the chaos of war, as happened in many European countries after the Second World War, but this need not happen. Discussion about constructive change can be encouraged and can go on all the time.

Radical ideas about community government, control of multi-national companies, a living wage for everyone, discussed during the past three or four decades in the six counties were never taken seriously by governments any more than any other suggested changes in our systems. Such unwillingness to discuss possible changes in our democratic systems leads to the suspicion that there may be unwillingness to accept democracy at all, since democratic government is always open to discussion about change.

Many people in Ireland reject democracy in their associations as well as in society as a whole. The churches, while some of them have elements of democratic government within themselves, have always had serious reservations about whether people in general should have democratic government. Democracy means that the will of the people should be fulfilled as effectively as possible but churches and other associations have often prevented this happening. Some of them say simply that they are not democracies themselves. Yet the Catholic Church claims that its members are inspired by the Holy Spirit. With members endowed like this it should be the greatest democracy in the world because everyone so inspired must have something wise to say. The political parties do not claim that their members are divinely inspired but have been forced to acknowledge that the people can vote wisely, while the church, which does claim its members are divinely inspired refuses to create structures which will enable them to say what they think.

At one end of the church spectrum the Presbyterian Church claims it is more democratic than others. But the history of the Presbyterian Church is one of great severity in its imposition of laws and rules even against the will of the people who had to live under them. The Calvinist Church in Geneva imposed fines on people who did not attend church and for other faults. The decision to govern in this way was not arrived at by the majority decision of the people most affected by it or by common consent or by enlightened discussion among the faithful at large. The even more severe decision that God decreed eternity in hell for people even before they were born was not arrived at through the deliberations of those affected spiritually and mentally by such a doctrine. People, the Geneva leaders believed, should have little say in their fate either in this world or in the next.

Presbyterian Church government is a different matter. The church has democratic structures and procedures. However, experience in the six counties has shown that the Presbyterian Church will enforce its laws and teachings through state or municipal laws, even if this affects people who are not members of this or any church. Presbyterian rules about Sunday observance for example are upheld by state laws which inflict penalties on those who disobey them whether these are church members or not.

Among religious groups, the Society of Friends has perhaps the greatest claim to having democratic forms in their assemblies. Clergy control of education in both jurisdictions in Ireland, insisted on by church leaders, and control of politics by clergy in the six counties, inhibit democracy, just as control of education and politics by any group in perpetuity would. There are other forms of educational and political management which would be effective and democratic.

The purges in the Irish Labour Party of the 1970s to exclude the radical left showed how a political party allows free expression as long as it accords with the ideology of the leaders. The purging process is similar in churches and political parties. The churches have their excommunication and heresy trials, political parties have purges.

In Britain and the United States in the 1980s there was a political onslaught on the trades unions which had been set up to give working people a voice. While trades unions were under this attack however they were eliminating their own radical left, just as were the labour parties which they supported. In a democracy such as we know it people with radical views or ideas may be allowed few opportunities to make their voices heard. Although freedom of speech is a principle of

143

democracy, depriving people of an opportunity to speak as they wish to is normal.

A journalist wrote in an Irish newspaper that Albert Reynolds had 'conferred respectability on Sinn Féin'. Sinn Féin received the votes of 12% of the people of the six counties, and represented between 35% and 40% of the Catholic population there. It was the largest nationalist party elected to Belfast city council. So the newspaper believed then that a party duly elected by a substantial number of people could be made 'respectable' by the intervention of someone not connected with the election or even living in the electoral area. The implied reason was that Sinn Féin had supported the right of people to armed revolution, in particular the armed revolution of the IRA.

Here a dilemma arises for democrats. For them it is the electors, the people, and they alone who are competent to decide whether a candidate or party is able and worthy to represent them. Political parties, churches, journalists and others may try to persuade people not to vote for one party or another, that is what election campaigns are about – but in the end it is left to the people to decide the rightness or wrongness, the suitability or otherwise of each candidate. To say that a duly elected person or party should be, or is, made politically respectable otherwise than by the votes of the people is to deny a fundamental principle of democracy. The will of the people must be respected. Their choice is already respectable.

No politicians or parties in Ireland refused to recognise and respect the Ulster Unionist Party although it had a 50 year record of unfair government, or Paisley's DUP although Paisley had a record of four decades of anti-Catholic campaigning. Neither the Unionist Party nor the DUP showed evidence that their behaviour would be different in the future but their acceptability to voters was recognised as their badge of respectability. In Britain and Ireland there was no suggestion that those who supported the Gulf war, or any other war, should be refused recognition or needed to be made respectable. Once the electors made their choice through a free vote their right to be heard through their representatives was recognised even if the representatives approved of unfair government, anti-Catholic campaigns and unnecessary war.

This right to fair representation, stated in the Irish Constitution of 1937, the Government of Ireland Act (1920), the United Nations Charter of Human Rights and the European Convention on Human Rights was accepted by Irish people in general as meaning that unionists and British representatives should be heard, no matter what their record had been. Once the people had spoken through the ballot box their right was absolute. This recognition however did not apply to all. In particular it did not apply to the freely chosen representatives of Catholics in the north-east. In December 1990 the SDLP was described in the Dáil as 'the legitimate and democratic representatives of the nationalist population in the North' at the time of the New Ireland Forum. While the Forum was sitting Sinn Féin obtained 43% of the Nationalist vote.

In Ireland it had been taken for granted in the past that communists should not be voted for, and if elected should not be given places as other elected representatives would. Few protested that this was similar to the rejection of Jews, Catholics or communists elsewhere and was indefensible. That no court action was taken by voters against such a defiance of law indicates that people believe democracy as we understand it need allow only a severely limited, provisional form of recognition for elected representatives – those elected will be heard provided government and other powerful bodies agree that they should.

Some elected representatives show that they reject basic democratic principle in the way they interpret their relationship with their voters and their party. When vigorous campaigns were going on against extradition of prisoners accused of political offences it became clear that most voters for Fianna Fáil were opposed to their extradition to a British jurisdiction. When elected representatives went from their constituencies to party meetings in Dublin, however, they found that the Fianna Fáil parliamentary party was in favour of extradition. So they rejected the decision of their electors and agreed to central party policy instead.

145

Síle de Valera acknowledged the dilemma. She knew, she said, that a majority of her voters were against extradition but when she came to Dublin found that official party policy was in favour of it, so she agreed with official party policy. 'That,' she remarked on a radio programme, 'is what democracy is about'. The elected representatives in this case of Fianna Fáil put into operation the wishes not of their voters but of their party when there was a difference between the two.

Public opinion polls showed that a majority of the electorate in the south were in favour of divorce but as time went on this apparent majority grew smaller until eventually voters in a referendum were split almost exactly for and against. But the proportion of elected representatives who worked and voted for divorce was larger than the proportion of their constituents who, according to the opinion polls and eventual referendum, wanted it. Most of the elected representatives supported party policy in favour of divorce but nearly half of those who elected them voted against it.

In the extradition controversy the elected representatives went against the wishes of their voters while in the divorce referendum nearly half the voters went against the advice and persuasion of their elected representatives. There is a quiet struggle for control of policy between cabinet and backbenchers and between voters and those they elect to represent them.

This poses a question about what representatives are elected to do. Are they elected to express in parliament the opinions and wishes of their voters and to make laws accordingly, or to create – or agree to – policies made by a small number of parliamentarians which they then try to persuade their voters to accept? Are they elected to express the opinions of their voters or to change them? Elected representatives will reflect the views of their voters, but policies will be created by a small number of people and the elected representatives instructed to persuade the voters that these policies should be made into law. This is the way the party system works and in a democracy of this kind there are few effective mechanisms for finding out what the voters' wishes are.

Whatever interpretation one puts on the meaning of elected representation – whether it is to reflect the wishes of voters or to persuade them to accept their party's policies or both – one may question the meaning and effectiveness of our parliamentary representation in modern conditions. Although people are more aware of political issues and have means of almost instant communication, we are still working on the democratic assumptions of many decades ago.

In the six counties a new structure of government must be created but this need not be, and arguably should not be, based upon old assumptions and practices. We could instead take this opportunity to rethink some of our assumptions and make more democratic and effective arrangements for Ireland as a whole now that we have the chance to do it.

If the model of parliamentary government which we inherited from Britain and is now past its useful life span is used once again, we shall have missed our opportunity to create a democratic system more advanced than any yet available in any country.

Although the Irish 1937 Constitution broke away from the British system to a degree it still accepted some of the assumptions of the British. It refused a state church and the right of a hereditary monarch or a house of unelected landowners to reject or inhibit the will of the people and in this it was an advance on the British system. But it kept the underlying presumption of the British that the people as a whole could not be trusted to make laws without being supervised by those who were seen as having special qualifications or special interests and therefore knew better. In the British system the supervision was crude, by a house of unelected aristocracy and an unelected hereditary royal house both of whom had to give their consent before the will of the people as expressed in their parliament could become law. In the course of time the power of the lords was reduced while the power of the monarch remained, restricted only by silent understandings that he or she would not go too far in restraining the will of the people.

In the Irish 1937 Constitution such crudities were rejected but an underlying assumption that the people as a whole could not be trusted to make good laws seemed to remain. Besides the Dáil, the parliament of the people's representatives, a second chamber or Senate (Seanad Éireann) was set up consisting of representatives of special interests, farmers, university graduates and people of other professions. Those who used to be referred to as 'the common people' could still not be trusted to make adequate laws for the whole community without being supervised by those presumed to know better or whose special interests had to be protected.

A difference between the British and the Irish system was that in Ireland both representatives and overseers were elected by the people, directly to the Dáil and the Presidency, indirectly to the Seanad, but the underlying presumption was similar – before the will of the people as expressed by representatives in the Dáil could become law, approval had to be asked for from the Seanad, who represented special interests, and the president. The Seanad had less power to delay laws than the British House of Lords whose powers have been curbed gradually during the past hundred years and no power to prevent them absolutely. But there is always the strong possibility of law being enacted through the interaction of strong interests among whom the people as a whole may play only a minor part.

Even in the United States, the 'common people' could not make laws without the intervention of an Upper House and the people's enactments can be vetoed by state and federal presidents. After the French Revolution whose rhetoric inspired other revolutions and killed princes it was only a few years until Napoleon was an emperor and kings were accepted once again.

It is said that our systems achieve the checks and balances needed in a democratic society. However, it must be asked whether in modern conditions checks and balances could not be inserted into the system in such a way as to make the will of the people, expressed through directly elected representatives, supreme and effective. A system in which all parties form a coalition, with independent deputies coalescing to take seats in government according to the number of votes they received, and government in place for a fixed period of four or five years might well provide such checks and balances. Such a new arrangement might at least make it clear that the will of the whole people, untrammelled by permission from special interests, or royal houses, or organised wealth and influence is accepted as the source of the people's laws. After the upheaval of the six counties when politicians must write a new Constitution the removal of old assumptions and the creation of new and more democratic principles should become possible.

New democratic arrangements in Ireland must involve a complete recognition of the right of all the people's representatives to have a voice in government. This right, never fully recognised in Ireland as a whole, was completely denied in the six counties. The Ulster Unionist Party operating a one party government unchangeable by democratic means was recognised as having a right to rule because it was supported by the votes of a great many people. It was criticised, condemned and eventually suspended because of its record of discriminatory behaviour which it was unwilling or unable to change, but there was no suggestion that the Ulster Unionist Party should be excluded from government in the future. The government in Dublin treated the Unionist Party with respect because of the large number of voters it represented.

Paisley's party, the DUP, was given similar recognition and respect and Catholics did not suggest that because of the party's anti-Catholic campaigns it should be set aside and unheard in discussions about a future democracy.

Many people therefore assumed that the fundamental democratic principle of recognising the people's elected representatives was accepted. They were wrong.

When Sinn Féin became an electoral threat to the SDLP in the early 1980s it became clear that the Dublin and London governments, the churches and nearly all newspapers and other media rejected the right of people to select their own representatives. Those who voted for Sinn Féin were told they were not going to be heard and Sinn Féin was not going to be recognised, no matter how many votes it got.

Democrats argued that the people, the voters, and they

alone were entitled to decide who should represent them. There is no indication in the Irish 1937 Constitution or the Government of Ireland Act (1920) that governments have a right to refuse to recognise the people's chosen representatives. The people's right to be heard through freely chosen representatives seems therefore to be officially accepted. The governments, churches, political parties and most journalists, however, believe otherwise: people have a right to elect only those candidates who are approved by government.

This denial has been seen in the broad political field and also in local disputes. When the dispute arose between the Orange Order and local residents at Drumcree in July 1996 the Order refused to deal with residents because, they said, one of their freely chosen representatives was a member of Sinn Féin. The same happened at Ormeau Road in Belfast where the Order rejected the chosen representatives of the local people and demanded that others, acceptable to the Order, should speak for them. This rejection of freely chosen representatives was encouraged by RUC, church leaders and politicians who urged that an independent body, not the local residents should decide the matters in dispute. As a last resort then, a dispute may be submitted to discussion between persons appointed by the government, not by the people. At much the same time an Irish semi-state company agreed to negotiations in an industrial dispute only if the representative chosen by the unions stood aside. These events showed how normal was the refusal to acknowledge the right of people to choose their own representatives at any level.

Those who denied people the right to elect representatives through whom they must be heard continued however to declare the need for democratic principle and freedom of speech. But Irish censorship showed they did not accept the democratic principle of freedom of speech either. The reason given for censorship on radio and television was that some people might use these media 'to advocate violence'. But if interviews were recorded, as most are, there was no possibility that any advocating violence would be transmitted. The governments were afraid not that elected representatives of the people would talk violence but that they would talk sense. When Sinn Féin and previously excluded community workers were eventually allowed on radio and television the public could understand, to the surprise of some of them, how justified the government's fears were.

Censorship and the exclusion of political parties by government decree showed that it would be impossible to create democracy in Ireland unless there was a significant change of attitude in governments and other institutions and in the public mind; a democracy cannot be founded on un-democratic principles.

The erosion of the authority of the law courts also showed how quickly and covertly democratic principles could be sub-verted. Taoiseach Jack Lynch questioned the result of the Arms Trial in which one of his ministers had been acquitted and said he was sure after all that a conspiracy to import arms did exist. James Kelly, one of the acquitted defendants wrote: 'The Taois-each was rejecting the court decision and impugning the integ-rity of the twelve jurymen'. He was also casting a shadow over the democratic principle that everyone is innocent until a duly constituted court declares him/her guilty and everyone has a right to be considered innocent until this is done. In the mean-time the way was opening gradually to a final rejection of the democratic principle of presumed innocence with demands that defendants be refused bail on the ground that they might commit 'further crimes' when they had not been proved to have committed the one of which they were accused. It seemed more and more that guilt or innocence could be declared with-out the stringent proofs which democratic courts should re-quire. A court could judge and have its judgement rejected by a Taoiseach. A police inspector could declare a person a sub-versive and have him imprisoned. The difference between the Taoiseach and the inspector was that the courts could imprison on the word of an inspector but not on the word of a Taoiseach.

The refusal of democracy is perhaps too deeply rooted, too pervasive and too widely approved in Irish society, to be chang-ed into acceptance in less than a few generations. The refusal of democracy is encouraged by the liberal press in Ireland.

# 12
## TRUTH IN THE NEWS

The Dublin based *Irish Times* published three articles on West Belfast which residents there complained misrepresented them and their way of life. They invited the journalists involved to come to Belfast to discuss them. Two journalists accepted the invitation. One of them was asked why in the articles describing West Belfast a young Catholic priest who had been in the area for two years and disliked it should be quoted about conditions there while residents who had lived in the area for 25 years were not asked their opinion. One of the journalists replied that the priest would be accepted by their readers as a credible witness, the residents would not. When it was pointed out that residents should be more credible witnesses about conditions in the area in which they had lived for 25 years, he replied that the *Irish Times* would publish what its readers wanted to read.

This confirmed the fears of people who had watched news reports about the six counties with dismay for many years. A newspaper will publish what its readers want to read but it will publish also what its advertisers and management want its readers to read. It may or may not be accurate. Journalists, it seems, learn what is acceptable to advertisers and management and hence to editors and tell their stories accordingly.

In the case of the *Irish Times* articles on West Belfast even the discreet reports sent in by journalists were adjusted by sub-editors before publication.

The problems which the resulting misinformation causes do not end with today's readers who are misled by news reports. In future years historians will look to contemporary newspapers as valid sources of information about what happened in the period they are studying. They may take for granted that the newspapers, or surviving television recordings, are accurate. But often they are not. They are a version of reality which accords with the needs of newspaper owners, readers, advertisers and political groups. There may be other and truer versions not available now or for future historians.

During the 25 years of war in the six counties some people became dismayed by the difference between what they saw on television or read in the newspapers and what they knew was happening in their streets and homes. The problem became apparent in the early 1970s. Readers of *Newsweek* and *Time Magazine*, published in the United States, had believed these magazines were giving them an accurate account of what was happening in, say, Korea or Khartoum. As the political situation developed in Belfast and Derry readers there realised that the *Time* and *Newsweek* accounts of what was happening in their streets were inaccurate and sometimes seriously misleading.

Some recalled what Claude Cockburn had written years before about reporting in the internal Spanish war of 1936–1939. Journalists 'covering' the Spanish war, he recalled, used to sit in cafes miles from the front and write their reports from there. Imagination was important, observation not necessary. But, Cockburn wrote, they had to be careful because Spaniards living in exile in England and elsewhere would recognise local inaccuracies if any occurred. It was important not to describe troops running down one street into another when Spaniards would know that one ran up that way into a street of another name. They achieved the necessary accuracy by using detailed maps of the areas where the fighting was taking place.

During the 25 year war in the six counties journalists working from the Europa Hotel and novelists specialising in quick selling novels set in contemporary trouble spots used the same methods. Novelists spent some weeks in Belfast or Derry to get the topography right and then wrote their stories in comfort. Journalists often based their stories on hand-outs, imagination and occasional visits to afflicted areas for local colour. Sometimes pictures were composed to make a useful television or newspaper scene. One of the frequently appearing pictures in newspaper reports of troubled areas is that of children holding guns. The message is that evil people are encouraging this among children while they skulk in the background themselves. Many trouble spots are reported to the accompaniment of such child pictures. In Belfast they were set up by photographers. Sometimes local residents stopped them.

A reporter tried to bribe a young girl to run towards a building in which a bomb was about to explode so that he could get what he considered an adequate picture. She refused. Another asked residents of an area under attack by loyalists to phone her 'at once if a child gets killed'. The manufacturing, adjustment and selection of news was necessary for the medium. It was accepted by some journalists that the function of news was to decide in advance what a story was about and find images to prove it.

People realised, then, that they needed their own networks of communication through which to tell people in other countries, and even in their own, what was really happening to them. They needed to give an accurate account to as many people in different parts of the world as would accept it, and build up an account of events which in years to come would give historians an alternative source to that of newspapers and commercial and official tapes.

In the six counties from the 1960s until the 1990s a mass of literature was produced by political groups, local associations and individuals. A collection of it is preserved in Belfast's Linenhall Library. Although this was freely available church officials and politicians often complained, 'We do not know what these people want'. During three decades people without an official voice had made their needs, suggestions, hopes and plans clear again and again. The problem was not that such people did not speak; it was that others did not listen.

In times of political upheaval the commercial media may not after all provide the vital stream of information which people need; they are censored and censor themselves. Pamphleteers, writers and distributors of single sheets of paper may do it. During the Second World War in occupied countries news sheets were printed in basements and flung into doorways by cyclists while the major newspapers were closed or censored into impotence.

In the six counties fax machines and computers opened up new possibilities for those who wanted to say their own words and provide an alternative to mass media which were often biased, often wrong and always commercial.

Information networks were created between Ireland, the United States, Canada, England, Australia, Continental Europe among people who were willing to receive alternative data and assess it for themselves. As these networks developed one small group in Belfast reckoned on reaching about 150,000 people a week. None of the commercial media could have offered such a service. In place of an occasional mention, possibly inaccurate, in the commercial media citizens had a regular means of communication over which they had control. It was a useful lesson on how dependency on mass media can be reduced by citizens determined enough to do it.

Although the most expensive technology was in the hands of the largest media owners, times were changing. Communication cannot exist without trust and credibility and as the conflict unfolded in the six counties trust in the media dwindled and, for many, disappeared. It was possible in the 1960s to say, 'I saw it on television' as a proof that what one said was true. Three decades later what was on television was seen as something about which one could be indignant, or disdainful, which one could agree with or not according to one's own judgement. People saw the media not as a means of communication only but as an instrument which could and should be manipulated by 'ordinary' people just as it was by those with power. Seen as an instrument to manipulate, the question was, who should manipulate it, and for 'ordinary' people, how could they do it?

As the commercial media have become concentrated into fewer hands, Berlusconi, Black, O'Reilly, Maxwell, Murdoch, there is increasing need for independent communication resources which will enable people to say to the mass media, Thank you, but we don't need you.

Media presenters and producers did not seem to realise how quickly and effectively that could happen as into the 1990s they became more and more intrusive, rhetorical and even abusive. Private citizens were getting access to more effective technology and media people were causing the indignation which would encourage them to use it.

In August 1995 a group of residents of West Belfast arranged a conference on 'The Democratisation of the Church(es)' to be held in Dublin in the following month. Most of the press ignored it, as they had ignored an initiative in 1990 by people in West Belfast who attracted 400 delegates from 16 countries to an international conference in the centre of Belfast on Irish democracy of the future. *The News of the World* Dublin edition of 3 September announced on its front page in an article by John Moore that the 1995 Dublin conference was organised 'by rebel priests who were going to defy the Pope by demanding the right to marry and have sex'.

The reality was that the conference was organised to bring people together to exchange views about the churches without having to listen to lectures, where the people who attended would be free to decide for themselves what should be talked about and how. There were no prearranged topics and everyone could speak who wanted to. Describing such a conference as a meeting of rebel priests defying Pope and Vatican and demanding sex might seem inexplicable.

But it is not.

Because most of the press ignored the 1990 conference in Belfast to discuss the shape of future democracy in Ireland many people did not know it was going on. Like the 1995 Dublin conference on the churches it was arranged by people who did not represent any church, political party or other institution. Although journalists often demanded democratisation in the state or the churches, by this they meant change brought about by the interaction of the institutions with each other, political parties, governments, churches, the press and others. 'Ordinary' people did not have any function in the matter apart from assenting to what was decided by the leaders of the institutions.

There is a widespread belief that there are classes in society who have the right and the ability to manage political, church or financial affairs and if others organise themselves to do such things they are suspect and what they do should be ignored or neutralised. As late as April 1996 it was still possible for a speaker on an RTE radio programme to talk about 'informing the masses' without being criticised for it. Dividing people into the elite and the masses did not disappear at the end of the nineteenth century as some may have suspected. 'Ordinary people' are still expected to recognise their position in society. Their opinions will not be accepted if they do not accord with what the press believe their readers want to read, or other institutional leaders want them to think. If they organise public meetings without the support of the institutions they will be at best ignored, at worst accused of being a front for subversives. We are still divided into classes, not only of the rich and the rest but of those who are permitted to make changes and those who are not. Private action to liberate a community from drugs may earn a prison sentence, to democratise the churches, public ridicule. Journalists or police may be the judges of which it will be.

Conway Mill, an old linen mill in West Belfast which had been vacant for some years, was opened as a community industrial and commercial development project in 1983. It was managed by people some of whom had been active in the Republican movement in the 1940s and 1950s. They rented the mill buildings from a social club affiliated to Sinn Féin and then bought it. The project became a limited company whose books were open to inspection by anyone, and they planned to create work spaces and support for 250 people. This would replace almost exactly the number of jobs lost when the mill closed.

The *Irish Times* published a story, that Conway Mill had been bought by the British government intending it for use by the local community but had been 'taken over' by Sinn Féin. The report was inaccurate. The building had never been owned by the government nor did they do anything to put it into the control of the local community. A club affiliated to Sinn Féin, named The Loney after the area in which it was located, needed new premises and bought the mill. It needed only part of the site with its complex of buildings, so it offered the rest for a nominal rent to be developed for community enterprise. The group who accepted the offer consisted mainly of Republicans who had been imprisoned, mostly by internment without trial, in the past.

One floor, about four thousand square feet, out of a total of about 100,000, was set aside for educational and cultural projects, including management courses, to be run rent-free by Springhill Community House, a registered educational charity. The rest of the space was to be used for industrial and commercial development by local people starting small businesses who could afford only small rents in an area of chronic unemployment.

The information that the complex was never in the possession of the British government and the government had never attempted to turn it over to the local community was available to the *Irish Times*. An account of the mill and the intentions and legal standing of its new developers had been delivered by hand to the media including the *Irish Times* a week before the story appeared. The reporter did not discuss it with any person involved in ownership or management of the mill.

The Management Committee of the mill was so angry it asked Douglas Gageby, *The Irish Times* editor, to meet them so that they could voice their concerns. He attended the meeting and was sympathetic to their complaints.

A few years after the new Management Committee had bought the mill, the French daily newspaper *Figaro* described an event which it said took place in Conway Mill in West Belfast. This, it said, was a meeting of chiefs of the IRA who vowed that the war must go on. The event never happened. What did happen was that a group of people who had been active in the Civil Rights movement in the 1960s met in the Mill Theatre to discuss what the Civil Rights movement had achieved and how it could continue to work for Civil Rights in the future. The meeting was attended by Michael Farrell, Bernadette McAliskey and others who later published an assessment of the Civil Rights situation as they saw it. No member of the Mill Management Committee or organiser of the Civil Rights meeting was interviewed for the *Figaro* story.

About the same time a newspaper in Melbourne, Australia published a similar story, again without interviewing anyone involved in the mill.

A British television company, Central Television, made a programme, *The Cook Report,* condemning Conway Mill as an IRA front. No members of the Management Committee were interviewed, nor any person working or studying there. A member of the SDLP, Dr Brian Feeney, head of a department in the local Catholic College for Teachers' Education managed by the Dominican Sisters was filmed standing in front of the mill speaking against it. Neither he nor Roger Cook who presented the programme discussed their allegations with any member of the Mill Management Committee.

Dr Feeney was aware of some of the work being done in the mill to provide adult education in an area where official provision was inadequate, including a campaign to persuade education authorities to set up a College of Further Education – a 'fourth college' – to fill the gaps in education for local adults. At this time Springhill House and Conway Mill were providing courses for adults as effectively as they could, helped by the Workers' Educational Association, the Arts Council, local education authorities and others.

Dr Feeney in a letter to *The Irish News* said it was desirable that the authorities should provide a fourth college because of 'dubious alternatives' which might be created if they did not. Those who worked in Springhill House and Conway Mill believed that their work would be among those described as 'dubious alternatives'. They were also independent.

The suggestion in *The Cook Report* was that the aim of Conway Mill was not social improvement or education but 'laundering' government funding for the IRA. The project's accounts were open to public view, however, and in any case the British government had given no money to it. Rental income was so small that the Management Committee could not employ necessary maintenance staff. Government assistance to employ workers under a community employment scheme had been stopped after one year. The project continued to exist because teachers and others worked without pay and donations were given by friends including some in the United States. In 1983 'The Doors of Hope' was founded in New Jersey to help this and other independent Irish enterprises.

It took five years and the surmounting of many legal obstacles before Central Television had to pay costs of about a million pounds. In December 1995 *The Guardian* published a story that Cook was 'in trouble again, this time over an unfair attack on a cancer specialist'.

Stories damaging to the Mill which appeared in different places were strikingly similar to each other. While the *Irish Times*, Central Television and others were alleging that Conway Mill was a IRA front, the education project there was the only place in Belfast from which invitations were sent out regularly to all political parties, including the Ulster Unionists and the Democratic Unionists to use the facilities of the Mill, especially during election times, where they were assured of a courteous reception. Because of government boycott and misrepresentations in the press and television fewer and fewer political groups accepted the invitation. Those who avoided the mill for political reasons then said they were right all along, nobody was using the mill except Sinn Féin and some radical socialist groups, so it must be an IRA front indeed.

Few groups were using the only place in the city which had an open door policy to encourage all political groups to use its facilities, including assembly hall, theatre, discussion rooms and crèche. Most others accepted false reports as true when they could have responded positively to a creative invitation during one of the most terrifying periods of Belfast's history. Media reports helped to ensure that they did not.

Clearly it was in someone's interest to tell people as far apart as Ireland, Britain, Australia and France that a project to create 250 jobs in West Belfast was an IRA front and should be destroyed. It is not clear who the originators of the reports were or whether they were intent upon undermining locally created enterprise or Sinn Féin or both. Whatever the origins, the resources to invent and plant such stories in the media are formidable. They recall the activities outlined by Colin Wallace and Fred Holroyd who created black propaganda for the British government in the 1970s, planting compromising stories to be picked by whoever was willing to believe them.

Why does a newspaper pretend a conference of concerned Christians about the democratisation of their churches is a sex conference organised by rebel priests? Why do an Irish newspaper, a French one, an Australian one and a British television company tell a strikingly similar untrue story without asking those most closely involved what the truth of the story is?

*The News of the World* deals in stories about sex and this may seem an adequate answer to the first question. But the paper can find stories of real sexual activities in Ireland without much difficulty. To turn the meaning of a story on its head and suggest a lie about it is unnecessary. The *Irish Times* and other newspapers have no sexual demands from their readers comparable to those from readers of *The News of the World*.

The media are a powerful weapon for governments and well resourced pressure groups. In the struggles for power in Ireland it is considered necessary to undermine those who try to make changes in society without having been authorised to do it by some powerful institution. *The News of the World*, the *Irish Times* and others are instruments of conservative institutions engaged in contests for power. 'Ordinary' citizens holding a conference to forward the ideals and understanding of democracy do not necessarily meet with the favour of the liberals. 'Ordinary' people should be taught rather than teach. Democracy defined by 'ordinary' people could be as dangerous to the institutions of church and state as any other form of subversion. Institutions, it is agreed, must be changed but they must be changed by their interaction with other institutions, otherwise the society constructed by the institutions for their own benefit may be destabilised.

A paper publishes what its readers wish to read. *The News of the World* judged that subversion of the meaning of a citizens' conference on democracy in the churches would be acceptable to its readers most of whom are probably conservative Irish Catholics. As are those of the *Irish Times*.

# 13
# STRUGGLES FOR POWER

There are struggles for power in Ireland as there are everywhere. In the six counties the clerical class has been powerful since the beginning of the state, threatening and subduing the politicians, nearly all of whom had to belong to religious secret societies in order to survive politically. Clerics controlled the largest political parties, most of the schooling and for a long time much of the welfare provision of the six county state. Democratic changes in the six county power structures in the future then must involve lessening the influence, power and wealth of the clerical class.

In 1996 a senior member of the Ulster Unionist Party suggested that the close links between his party and the church-based Orange Order should be loosened. About one-third of the Ulster Unionist Council, the policy-making body of the party, are delegates from the Orange Order. This change would shift the balance of power between clergy and politicians in the party and was resisted by the leader of the order, Martin Smyth, a Presbyterian clergyman and member of the Westminster parliament. The movement towards loosening the links between the Orange Order and the Unionist Party was supported by the Drumcree Group who believe that neither the order under its present leadership nor the Ulster Unionist Party are vigorous enough in their opposition to Catholic demands and to British policy. At a meeting in Belfast's Ulster Hall they demanded that the Orange Order's supreme ruling body should be elected democratically by all the order's members and that the links between the order and the Unionist Party should be lessened.

The Drumcree Group believe this would enable the order to act more militantly without being inhibited by what they consider an ageing and ineffective leadership. It would be able to act as a stronger political pressure group independently of the party. They believe the order must resist British and even

Unionist Party policy at a time when Trimble and others realise, as O'Neill realised in the 1960s, that the Unionist Party will
need the support of some Catholics if it is to survive.

Catholic membership of the Unionist Party would not be
tolerated by the Orange Order which has a dominating influence on unionist policies. Breaking the connection between
Orangeism and the party would enable the party to invite Catholics to join, while the order itself would then become more
independent and therefore stronger opponents of Civil Rights
for Catholics. In other words, breaking the Orange–unionist
link would enable the unionists to induct Catholics into support for the state while strengthening the ability of the Orange
Order to threaten those who refused the invitation and contain
the influence of those who accepted it.

In the south clerical power was institutionalised by law in
the education, welfare and health systems but not in the political system, while in the six counties clerical power was institutionalised in politics as well as education and welfare.

In the south there is nothing corresponding to the Ulster
Unionist Council in which a religious society has seats by right
and therefore a large part in forming political party policy. This
policy-making council of the biggest unionist party, the Ulster
Unionist Party, is composed largely of men who have made a
solemn avowal that they are 'of Protestant parents, educated in
the Protestant Faith, and have never been in any way connected with the Church of Rome' and who also undertake not to
visit Catholic public houses or Catholic worship. Among the
members of the council not officially delegated by Orange
societies many are personally members of the order, whose
membership is open only to church-going Protestants.

There is no equivalent in the south of the Democratic Ulster
Party led by clerics.

The Catholic/Protestant analysis of the six county situation makes it appear that there are two religious groups more
or less equal in power and method fighting each other but
while clerical control of public affairs is often described as a
problem in the south it seldom is in the six counties. In reality,
with most schools, two major political parties and other in-

stitutions controlled by clergy, the six counties are the most clerically controlled region in the European Union.

They are also one of the least developed.

There are antagonisms and manoeuvring for power within the main Christian blocs. In the Catholic community there is a long-standing antagonism between nationalist politicians and clergy on the one hand and republicans or socialists on the other. Nationalists and clergy have often identified their main problem not as the British administration – whose social philosophy is much the same as their own, and who can, they believe, be brought round by persuasion to concede democratic government and even independence – but as the republicans and socialists. When Catholic Church leaders condemned the IRA and Sinn Féin during the 25 years of war they were echoing condemnations and analyses uttered many times before. They said in effect that Irish people were on the way to democracy, or peace, or even a United Ireland if republicans had not started a campaign of violence. Nationalists made the same charges against republicans involved in the 1916 revolution. John Redmond said in the British House of Commons:

> My first feeling, of course, on hearing of this insane movement was one of horror, discouragement, almost despair. I asked myself whether Ireland, as so often before in her tragic history, was to dash the cup of liberty from her lips. Was the insanity of a small section of her people once again to turn all her marvellous victories of the last few years into irreparable defeat, and to send her back, on the very eve of the final recognition as a free nation, into another night of slavery, incalculable suffering, weary and uncertain struggle. That doctrine has been contested by the same men who today have tried to make Ireland the cat's paw of Germany. In all our long and successful struggle to obtain Home Rule we have been thwarted and opposed by that same section. We have won Home Rule, not through them, but in spite of them. This wicked move of theirs was the last blow at Home Rule. It was not half as much treason to the cause of the Allies as treason to the cause of Home Rule.[1]

There is little evidence to support such self-confidence or condemnation of others. The evidence shows that successive British governments were determined to remain in control in part of Ireland; in 1995 John Major the British prime minister declared himself for the union.

Even when it was clear that the union could be maintained only at the cost of continuing undemocratic rule and enforced inequality, many nationalists still maintained it was republicans and not British governments who prevented Irish independence. The SDLP and the southern parties, church spokesmen and others said that the British government, in spite of its own declarations about it, was neutral.

The bitter anger between those who relied upon eventual British goodwill and those who said force must be used to win democracy in face of British intransigence had been proved during the civil war in the south in the 1920s. Atrocities were committed and an Irish administration in Dublin killed its prisoners. If a communist government killed its prisoners a decade later spokespersons for Catholic Ireland would have professed to be shocked – at the time they were shocked even by reports of nude bathing in Russia – but when the British and Irish administrations did it public conscience managed to accommodate itself to the fact. Such was the anger of the times that killing prisoners caused little effective public opposition.

Present antagonism between southern political parties is often bitter and is traced back, accurately or not but frequently, to the civil war, as Austin Deasy said in April 1996. Problems of unresolved anger between groups who believe their safety lies only in getting power for themselves are not peculiar to Ireland. The Spanish internal war in the 1930s intensified similar bitterness and left similar scars which are healing slowly now after sixty years.

Within the Catholic Church tensions stem from two interpretations of what 'Catholic' means. One view is that 'Catholic' means not only that Catholicism is for everyone all over the world but also that everyone in the church should think, say and believe the same things. This view was implied in Cardinal Daly's explanation of why he rebuked fellow bishops who said clerical celibacy could be voluntary. 'People need guidance and help', the *Irish Times* reported him as saying, 'in trying to discern what is the authentic position of the Catholic Church in the midst of a certain confusion'.

This statement reflects the view that since Catholic means all believing and acting in unison, it is important to avoid confusion. There is one way, one law, one form of worship and members of the church must conform to it and its leaders must define it; they believe it is contrary to the definition of Catholicism to allow differences to emerge because this causes confusion.

The other view is that Catholic means, among other things, being able to entertain and accommodate different views and practices. Statements by Cardinal Daly and other church leaders show that the single-mind view of Catholicism is uppermost in Ireland in the 1990s although dissenting voices are now raised more confidently than in the past.

Bishops believe confusion must be avoided and confusion is created by expressing differing views. Any deviation from what church leaders teach must then be avoided; if not there will be more than one voice about any topic.

In the Catholic Church however, members do have significantly differing views. There are differing views among members of a congregation who share the Eucharist at Sunday Mass. Some believe private property is held by divine permission, there is a divine right to property, and this right must be defended by the church. Others believe property should be shared because God meant the goods of the earth for the support and delight of everyone, that adequate sharing should be enforced by law if necessary and such sharing should be directed towards equalising means and opportunities for everyone. This is a significant difference of opinion among Christians about God's purposes and therefore about God and God's creation and our duty to both.

When a congregation says, 'We believe in God', different members have different views of what and whom they mean. For some, God is a fatherly but severe person. For others God has what they see as masculine qualities but is full of love and forgiveness in which severity plays no part. For others God can be understood only with reference to both male and female qualities. Others say such qualities are irrelevant and God is understood as pure spirit and will.

These are significant differences of understanding among Christians. For some Catholics, everyone must believe the same things, say the same things, worship the same way, use the same terms, put moral principles into practice in the same way. For others, the name Catholic means that the church is capable in a very special way of keeping its members united even when they have different views about what they believe, or how to interpret moral laws, about the meaning of life and many other matters. The first of these interpretations of what 'Catholic' means leads to strictness, exclusiveness, worry and sometimes cruelty. The second opens a way to a rich experience of religious life and in particular to a rich experience of the meaning of the Christian Eucharist.

In Ireland in the 1990s the dominant official Catholic view was that every Catholic should speak, worship and behave alike. Those who thought differently might no longer be penalised for it but should keep silent about it. Fr Kevin Hegarty was removed from editorship of the Catholic magazine *Intercom* in 1995 and replaced by a more conservative priest. Catholic belief was being publicly defined not only by those in positions of authority, but more and more by pressure groups prepared to take to the streets to impress on the public that there was only one authentic Catholic belief about moral behaviour.

In the six counties, strict single-view Christians who had been dominant for decades approached the year 2000 showing no sign of reducing their efforts or their power. For them the Sabbath was to be observed even to the point of destruction, homosexuality was evil in itself, drinking and dancing not only to be avoided by oneself but forbidden to others, sex was a manifestation of the fallen nature of men, women and children and a source of evil in its possessor more potent than firearms or money. Some professed to use sex only as a strict necessity but took eagerly to money and firearms and made a virtue of possessing them. In this transferring of esteem from God's creations for life to human beings' creations for death they were following an unhappy Christian tradition and Christians in Ireland encouraged such distortions of their faith less perhaps out of fear of God than out of fear of being condemned by their fellow Christians.

In the south during the disputes about abortion and divorce small groups took over leadership of Catholic opinion and misinterpreted Catholic beliefs and practices which had taken nearly two thousand years to evolve. At times during those 2,000 years of evolution Christians had believed and taught that men, women and even children could be killed for stealing or witchcraft or for being homosexual. They believed they had a God-given command to kill those who killed. With such a tradition of condoning and causing killing, Christians should be cautious about claiming to defend the absolute right to life of foetuses, but small groups of church members at official and street level proclaimed not only that human beings had a right to life but fertilised ova had it as well. Christians who accepted capital punishment and war in defence of property said that an ovum just after fertilisation was a special case and could never be killed. Many Christians in Ireland share this view, but Christian tradition has not been so demanding about human life.

Investing a fertilised ovum with individual human life is not entirely in accord with Christian tradition. Thomas Aquinas, the founder of Catholic, scholastic, philosophy, taught that a human soul is infused into a foetus only after about the third month of pregnancy. Abortion during this period he would have said then is wrong but not so wrong as abortion in later stages of pregnancy. During the first three months the abortion could not strictly speaking be called murder. After this period it could.

In the rhetoric of the streets this distinction was not made known although it was part of Catholic tradition. The banners proclaimed that every fertilised ovum was a human being and killing it was murder. Catholic leaders and theology teachers for whom Aquinas was the touchstone of orthodoxy did not dare point out what Catholic tradition really was. In the south it had become more dangerous to oppose religious pressure groups than to oppose religious leaders. Dissenters risked loss of prestige, position and in the six counties even life. Christians could prove formidable opponents.

A possible course for Christians who wanted a solution which was traditionally Christian and humane would have been to declare themselves committed to the preservation of human life in all its forms and at all its stages, while at the same time acknowledging that others might adopt either a severe view or a less severe one and still remain true to Christian traditions.

Although the single-view Christians have prevailed for decades in Ireland and elsewhere, it is not possible completely to submerge traditions which have been evolving for 2,000 years. In Germany, Italy and Poland modern lawmakers have made the distinction between a foetus before three months and after. In Germany they said that while abortion in the first period was illegal it would not be punished. Had this happened in Ireland it might well have been called derisively 'an Irish solution to an Irish problem' by commentators who refuse to recognise that Irish people solve problems much as others do, sometimes with special insight, sometimes not, but always with much the same reasoning. In Germany it was a traditional solution to a distressing and perennial problem in accordance with a traditional Christian balance between the ideal and the obtainable.

In Ireland as elsewhere the single-view Christians took over moral leadership when important moral problems were discussed, giving the impression that there was only one Christian answer when there could well be several.

Christians interpret their Eucharist in different ways – a commemoration, the real presence, a renewal of sacrifice – and these differences exist not only among theologians but also among members of congregations who share their Eucharist every Sunday. The differences do not result in crisis or in the paralysing confusion feared by the leaders, partly because they are not often spoken about. The strategy of trying to promote unity by silencing all opinions except one is an unproductive one however. It may prevent confusion in the conversation of church members but does not prevent the confusion which exists in their minds, a confusion which could disappear when people realise that it is normal and Christian to differ about the meaning of God and life and death. It is the internal repression of difference and the external repression of exchange of views that may lead to confusion and alienation. The result of these is not Christian unity born out of respect and reverence but Christian assent born out of fear. The significance and power of the Christian Eucharist is diminished by it.

One of the most significant policies of the Christians in Ireland has been their refusal to share their Eucharist. They say they cannot do this until all believe the same things about it. The contrary view is that we share our Eucharist as a way of becoming united. After all, we share the Eucharist with members of our own churches who have widely differing views about what it means.

The greatest characteristic and power of the church, the wide view Christians would say, is its ability to unite people who have such differing views, not only keeping them from arguing destructively but allowing them to argue while at the same time uniting them in their acceptance of Christ and each other, an acceptance symbolised in their Eucharist. There are many nuances, differences and even contradictions among Christians of any congregation and there are few organisations in the world where so many different views can be reconciled in such a powerful symbol of shared affection and respect as the Christian Eucharist.

The wide view of Catholicism is richer, less disturbing and closer to what Jesus Christ envisaged for his kingdom. There are many houses in his campus, many rooms in his house, but the more strict a Christian regime becomes the more people are excluded from them. If Jesus Christ had wanted an exclusive kingdom he would have said not that there were many rooms in God's house but that there were few and we must compete with each other to get in.

The wide view Christians neither welcome confusion nor fear it. They believe confusion is lessened, not increased, by discussion. They welcome not the confusion but the process by which they welcome those who differ from them without respecting them less. They welcome discussion, believing that the Christian community can help to create or revive the techniques of discussing anything with profound respect for everyone. They believe that this technique has been lost for too long.

For many decades the one-view Christians have ruled the Irish churches in private and public but this need not remain so in the future. One can argue that unless Irish Christians make dramatic and startling changes in their attitudes and relationships with each other and with their fellow citizens they will sink further into an irrelevance which, if it remains allied to wealth and political power, will become offensive as well as useless. If however the horizons are widened and fresh meanings are explored for Christian beliefs then Christians could have something significant to offer a world which needs the benefit of their 2,000 years' experience.

While Fr Michael Hurley said we should welcome 'mixed' marriages others insisted that toleration was a miserable thing and to aim at it only was to be satisfied with a minimal and mean recognition of our fellow citizens. We need our fellow citizens too much to be satisfied with tolerating them – we need their help, the experience of the Jews, the Muslims, atheists, socialists, communists, humanists, people of all traditions. Life is too difficult and too promising for us to attempt to live it alone.

Schemes to induce toleration will not help us to solve the conflict or heal the wounds which bad government and mean religion have caused. We need to make a bold leap forward which would fulfil Christ's prophecy: I have done great things but you will do even greater. We can understand the Christians who think only in terms of a church which has one rule, one way, one method, one set of beliefs and who therefore insist that those who deviate even by posing questions are offensive to the Christian community. But we have allowed them too much influence. Protestants and Catholics who married each other sometimes had their homes burned or one of the spouses murdered, or both of them driven into exile. A Jewish boy intending to marry a Christian could be cut off from his family by a ceremony which was like a funeral, because it marked a final break between them. A Muslim refuses to eat ham but employs children at £7.50 for ten and a half hours work every day of the week. It is difficult to see how people who cling to such beliefs and practices can have any creative place in making our future but their experience and that of those who deal with them must serve not as a model but as a warning that sometimes the best we can do for people is help them defend themselves against their institutions, even the best of them.

# 14

# PEACE AND PEACEMAKERS

In the six counties there is little room for pacifists. They were popular in the six counties between the two world wars but when the Second World War broke out pacifists everywhere became public enemies and some were beaten outside Belfast City Hall. Most of those who had declared themselves pacifists decided to support the war after all. Peace groups set up during peacetime can be numerous but volatile; those set up in time of war need to be exceptionally courageous – or not pacifist. Irish peace groups which appeared during the 25 years of war were not necessarily pacifist.

Two clergymen, a Catholic and an Anglican from Belfast were invited to address a peace group in Athlone. The peace group, they found to their surprise, was run by local army officers and their wives. Working for peace in this context did not seem to require a philosophy of pacifism. The two clergymen wanted to discuss the real causes of conflict, how governments lead people to war, not the other way about. They wanted to discuss how the people's resources are distributed and used by those who have power. This caused tension between them and the members of the peace group. They were asked not to discuss anything like this which might split the local peace movement.

During the meeting one of them referred to what was happening in the north-east as 'a war'. Some members objected to this, saying that calling it a war made respectable what was after all only a sectarian squabble. The speaker replied that there must be a fundamental difference between them if they believed war was respectable or waging war a respectable thing to do. A peace group which believes war is 'respectable' is not pacifist. It is concerned primarily with law and order enforcement and the defeat of political movements which it considers subversive.

There is a difference between pacifists and peace organisers. Rev. Donald Gillies, a Presbyterian minister in Belfast, reflected the thinking of Christian peace organisers when he said it is the duty of the state, using the police and military, to create a strong framework of law and order within which Christians will be able to act in a charitable and virtuous fashion towards each other. Showing love and respect to each other does not, they believe, bring peace. The Christians need the state to establish a framework of law and order in which they will be free to be virtuous.

Some years later Christians who said this also said, inconsistently, that people in the north-east could not create political structures – or have them created for them – until they had achieved peace and reconciliation. That is, peace and reconciliation would have to come first, then suitable institutions of government, including policing, soldiery and courts could follow. The two ideas are contradictory and yet were expressed by the same people. Christians explaining their failure to act charitably towards each other said they needed a political structure imposing law and order within which to do it. Christians explaining why we could not have suitable political structures said we needed to be at peace and reconciled to each other before we could create such political arrangements. Both arguments were in effect a refusal of substantial social change.

Christian leaders in Ireland who argued that only strong government would create the climate for peaceful co-existence gave almost complete support to police and military. They argued that given such support they could suppress opposition to government and thereafter, this work having been done, police and military would be needed less and less. A stable society could thus be created at the cost of suppressing those who opposed its excesses.

While thus supporting what had been state policy from the beginning Christian groups were reluctant to criticise even the excesses of police and military. At the same time they helped to create peace groups, reconciliation groups and cross community groups, all of which did worthy things but most of which reinforced the idea that political arrangements must be delayed until the citizens were at peace with each other. But even the Christians who said such things could hardly have believed that real politics could wait that long.

During the 25 year war the definition of pacifism became simply a condemnation of citizens' armed groups. Those who declared themselves pacifists were commanded to condemn the IRA or loyalist armed groups. If they refused, on the ground that their aim was to create peace rather than to make themselves appear respectable, they were condemned as 'fellow travellers with the men of violence'. In Ireland there has been little intellectually based discussion of what pacifism means – or of what violence means – in spite of the ravages of the war.

Peace groups were inhibited by discussions about community relations rather than peace, refusing to acknowledge that the stability which traders demanded, the law and order which the state demanded, and the quiet obedience which the churchmen demanded were likely in a politically developing community to lead not to peace but to revolution. A speaker invited to address members of the Peace People in Belfast was startled to be interrupted after five minutes by people who said, 'You are talking to us as if we were pacifists; we are not'. Many people who wanted peace believed that peace could be achieved only by defeating their opponents.

Those who come from the Judeo/Christian tradition, as most people in the six counties do, are at a disadvantage in making peace. The first books of their Bible created an image of God like that of an eastern potentate, killing or sparing with a word or a nod, fickle, fierce and demanding to be placated. The basic documents of this tradition give approval to violence including the relegation of women and others to a position of inferiority and even bondage. Some who belong to this tradition say that the message of Jesus Christ exorcised their violent ghosts, that with him a new era of peace and love replaced all that. History proves that this was not so and Jacques Maritain had reason to say sadly that he was less worried by the gibbets erected before Christ than by the multitudes of them erected after. The Christians did not at any time usher in an era of peace, justice and love. They were always promising to do it, though.

Until the Christians in Ireland and elsewhere remove the violence of their basic documents and turn away from their own violence and injustice, vowing never to repeat it, they will never make peace. Peace is not the work of people who believe in an arbitrary god who kills or spares with a nod, rewards or condemns even before his subject is born, who demands vengeance not only for doing what you do but for being what you are. Such a god presides over the thoughts of many of our citizens. They are entitled to their beliefs; but others are entitled not to be damaged by them.

For some the answer to the problem of powerful Christians, without whose approval no peace formula can work and without whose assistance no civil disturbance has ever been tried, is to demand a secular society. This would involve dismantling many laws and customs. There would be a restructuring of education, political parties would have to cease relying on clerical support and rely instead only on their own voters. Powerful religious societies would need to have their power defined and if necessary curbed. Laws regulating recognition of marriage or acceptance of moral principles would have to be revised. Those who recommend such changes will remember that each of them has at some time in history produced upheaval and sometimes bloodshed.

In the future it is business people rather than idealists who may have the greatest influence in creating a settlement in Ireland. When Charles Haughey was active in politics he recognised this, just as other business people like Albert Reynolds recognised it. On one enlightening occasion Charles Haughey addressed a meeting of business people in Belfast's Europa Hotel. His message was that modern business needed cooperation and stability, maximising internal Irish trade and creating a harmonious all-island setting for industry and commerce. Outside the hotel a Protestant clergyman, Ian Paisley, demonstrated with a handful of followers about religion and the encroachments of popery.

Charles Haughey got a standing ovation. People passed Paisley by.

It was a parable of the reality of the six counties where business is what it has always been about.

# Postscript

The IRA ceasefire broke after 18 months with the bombing of Canary Wharf in London. Loyalists and unionists in Ireland had been in disarray as long as the IRA ceasefire lasted. They felt sure of their ground while the war was on, they could define their politics by opposition to the war. But with the ceasefire in place they were called upon to make serious suggestions about permanent peace and a settlement, even an internal one. This made them profoundly uncomfortable. They laid down impossible conditions, the destruction of the republican movement, the giving up of arms, elimination of the Dublin government from the discussion, acceptance by the Westminster government of all unionist or loyalist demands, and control of police.

Their public representatives had no practice in serious discussion of political or economic issues. Even if competent negotiators were available to the unionist and loyalist groups these could be controlled and possibly neutralised by the organisations which had given them power, principally the Orange Order and the churches. For the unionists, being forced into discussions of any kind was a defeat, no matter what the issue or the outcome might be. In July 1997 even if Orange parades were allowed to march into Catholic areas there was an element of defeat in their right to do it being challenged at all. It would be a much greater defeat to have to ask permission from Catholic residents beforehand. A bitter dispute about Orange marches on the Garvaghy Road showed the divisions within the religious orders between those who were willing to make some compromises to save businesses and reputations and those who were not. The British government tried to persuade Orangemen to discuss their marching, however trivial this issue might be, with their Catholic fellow citizens. The Orangemen knew however that if they were forced to discuss this issue now they would be forced to discuss other more important issues later.

This they were unwilling to do. The unionist doctrine of 'Not an Inch' referred not only to their unwillingness in the 1920s to give up territory but also to their belief that if a concession of any kind and however small were given, all would be lost. Lose Ireland, lose the empire, lose Derry, lose 'Ulster', discuss anything, lose all. It was difficult for anyone outside the six counties to understand what the refusal to discuss small issues meant for the six county unionist. It was easy to ascribe it to blind bigotry. For the unionists it was not blind bigotry but political sense.

They did not accept that as circumstances changed they did not lose Derry, everybody gained it, they did not lose all but shared everything. There was no such political concept among unionists apart from a few whose voices were seldom raised. Many clergymen and others who might have moderated the Orangemen's attitudes fell silent and even seemed to encourage them in their determination not to give their inch.

The unionists then did not want to construct a coherent political philosophy and a programme which would carry them successfully through discussions, with stated principles, fall-back positions, etc. They wanted to avoid getting into discussions at all or at least to postpone them as long as possible. The most they would concede was that they should return to majority government allowing Catholics to sit on committees administering laws which they would never have any part in making. The Liberal Democrats in Britain found this an attractive idea and it remained the unionist position during the war and the ceasefire and the renewal of the war.

Unionist refusal to discuss with opponents has important reasons – inability to discuss, lack of experience in the building or working of democracy, and since they have experience only of one party government, their lack of the skills of compromise which political parties learn in order to maintain power. The politics of unionist inability led to the politics of unionist abuse until the normal approach of unionist politicians to those who disagreed with them or even wanted to talk to them was personal abuse. President Clinton, George Mitchell, Cardinal Daly, Ted Kennedy, John Hume, Irish and international politicians, the Pope and President Robinson have been attacked by them in a programme of abuse unique in European political life. The events of 1997 underlined this aspect of unionist political method. As the history of the early years of the six county state is more closely and dispassionately studied it may appear that abusiveness of this kind was not the policy of all the members of the original government but something they were led into by those who controlled them, principally their churches and secret societies.

In the 1920s those in the Unionist Party who wanted to create government which would be fair to all including Catholics were defeated by those whose main political objective was to curb Catholic power at all costs. In 1997 as the unionist factions fought their battles over street marches it seemed that those who wanted to win Catholics over to the unionist side might well win in the long run over those who wanted Catholics to be powerless, ghettoised and if possible expelled. The events of Drumcree and the intransigence within the secret societies had shamed even the respectable into some desire for change, unwelcome though it might be. The business people and church leaders among them had resources which in the long term would probably win. The increasing Catholic population had more economic and political power than at any time since the 1920s and showed signs of being impossible to curb any longer. Business and religious respectability required new doctrines and new methods but these could come into play only if the instruments which brought the rich and religious to power were blunted. The secret societies had to be brought under control.

While politicians in the rest of Europe were discussing their economies, social conditions or global survival, politicians in the six counties were discussing whether a church parade should stride up or down the Garvaghy Road and whether elected representatives should be heard or not and whether women were fit for public office and whether the Bible condemned their citizens who were homosexual. While the European Union was maturing for good or ill Ireland's north-east was condemned to perpetual childhood in which peace was sought by letting off balloons and riding in trains, and a British prime minister was led to try to solve its problems by a letter from a 12 year old girl while his attendance at a world conference was encouraged, he said, by his children. In a world where leaders refused to grow up, the creation of a modern democracy seemed by 1997 to be further off than ever, not through accidents of history but through incompetence of government.

Church officials and others had said that the obstacle to Sinn Féin being included in talks was the IRA offensive. None of them said however that if the offensive stopped Sinn Féin would be admitted. Britain's Conservative government gave no assurances at all, while the British Labour Party newly elected to government said that if the IRA ceasefire was reinstated Sinn Féin could be – not would be, but could be – admitted to talks. None of them even now recognised the absolute right of the people to elect their own representatives. The decision as to when Irish elected representatives would be admitted to talks about their people's future would rest as always with the British government and not the Irish electors. Refusal of the democratic principle that the people decide who shall talk on their behalf was still as remote from British and Irish political life as ever.

Ted Kennedy tried to break the impasse by saying that the British ought to make a firm commitment to a date for talks if an IRA ceasefire occurred. For those who had said months beforehand that any assurances from the British government would have to be underwritten by an internationally credible third party before they could be accepted, Ted Kennedy was going part of the way in asking for a public declaration from the British which would be hard to go back on. There remained a strong suspicion that those who most insistently demanded a renewed ceasefire – the British government and its Irish supporters – would still not know what to do with it if it happened. For those who wanted a ceasefire and negotiations because it was democratically right to have them, the need for an internationally credible arbiter was clear and there was no sign that the Dublin administration could or would fulfil this role. The time was approaching when the Dublin and London governments would make an agreement which they would then present to the people of Ireland for acceptance. It would be one of the least desirable of all solutions since the people who had suffered most would be excluded from making it, the six county unionists because of their inabilities, the six county nationalists and republicans because their right to make such plans was never fully recognised.

Meanwhile experience showed how flawed the British fair employment legislation for the six counties was – it needed only one employee of a company, one group of people at Harryville, one gathering of Orangemen at Drumcree, one section of the RUC, one government minister to disobey and the laws fell apart. Bushmills Distillery, the Harryville picket, Drumcree, the petty harassments in the ministry of agriculture, all taught the same lesson: the fair employment laws might ensure that aggrieved persons could get some money but they would not get their rightful job, and the simplest defiance of the laws would render those in authority powerless, from the secretary of state to the head of the RUC.

The longer the governments failed to address the real problems and concentrated on the secondary or tertiary problem of community relations the more grave the situation became. Even while the crisis was growing in July 1997 church leaders and governments were appealing for improvements in community relations among 'ordinary' people which they must have known could not be brought about without radical reforming action by government, no matter how willing the 'ordinary' people might be.

As the 1990s progressed the principles by which the area was governed came more and more into focus. The problem as seen by the two governments in Dublin and London was not to eliminate violence but to control the use of it. This struggle for control was now leading the British government and the RUC into conflict with their own most ardent supporters. Neither side in this struggle had the diplomatic skills to prevent it developing, both relying on the threat of more effective force to make sure it developed in their favour. This brought the religious loyal Orders into a position which their sponsors wished to avoid, fraternal contention in public.

The doctrine of the state's right to a monopoly of force continued to result both in government resistance to groups of Catholics organised to defend their districts and in the RUC confrontation with demonstrators threatening a Catholic church at Harryville. The problem for both government and police was not to eliminate violence but to decide who shall use it.

The loyalist and unionist population is experiencing struggles for power on a number of fronts, the Ulster Unionist Party against the Democratic Unionist Party in the elections in East and North Belfast for example. The Orange and other religious Orders are more and more divided as some members believe their interests will not be protected by the present leadership and want to take control.

The attitudes of Christians remained fixed during the war, during the ceasefires and afterwards. In the 26 counties a proposed new education bill illustrated some of their attitudes and fears. There was some clerical reaction against proposals towards declericalising education in the south. On the other hand, the bill proposed that school managements should have power to exclude teachers or pupils who would not uphold the ethos of the schools; teachers reacted against this. Between the 1920s and 1940s in the six counties the Protestant Churches and the Orange Order had struggled with their government about the same issues.

By a curious twist of logic people who said the republican movement is Catholic although it is not led by Catholic clergy believe that schools can be truly Catholic or Protestant only if led by clergy. Catholic Church officials in the south opposing the declericalising of education in the 1990s are weaker than the Protestant clergy in the six counties were during their early struggles for control of education. They may become stronger however, if people's fears are aroused about education, abortion, family values and law and order. The combination of Fianna Fáil, Progressive Democrats, church officials and others on such issues shows that disagreement on lesser issues can be buried when the control of resources for education, health or enforcement of the state's laws is at stake. Curiously, as public discussion of law and order develops, the Christians who most strongly uphold the philosophy of Christ in some things are most forward in advocating the building of more prisons as an answer to social problems even though Christ said that one of the signs of the authenticity of His mission would be that prisoners would be released. His most vigorous followers now say there should be more prisons and more prisoners in order to build a Christian society.

This reversal of Christ is not strange or unusual. What is strange is that it has not been challenged by any senior religious spokespersons any more than the existence and development of an armaments factory in Belfast were in the midst of a disastrous revolutionary war or the placing of Irish troops under NATO command in Bosnia in 1997. There are political and economic matters about which the Christians judge Christ to be incompetent.

The American government welcomed the IRA ceasefire partly or mostly because Ireland was a good place to do business. The ending of the IRA ceasefire put this in danger. But the continued involvement of Mr Mitchell the American chairman of the sterile forum discussions indicated that American policy was to placate the unionists, or loyalists, in the hope that they could be persuaded to negotiate. It was also to uphold British policy in Ireland and to help weaken the thrust of the republican movement. A number of difficulties will arise from this American government policy.

As American business interests become more involved in Ireland there will be an increasing demand for Americans to intervene if the struggle for human rights in Ireland is intensified. As in other areas, Americans could be urged to intervene diplomatically, financially or militarily in Ireland in defence of trading interests. Increasing American investment in the six counties together with United States government support of the British regime is a dangerous mixture which, if the British do not concede democratic government could lead to future disaster, with American as well as British and Irish governments involved. It is in the interest of Irish people as a whole that this should not be allowed to happen.

In such a situation, if the British government is unwilling to concede democratic government the American government will be seen to be supporting an undemocratic regime in Ireland, just as it has supported undemocratic regimes elsewhere. Already it has shown almost total support for British policy in Ireland against the wishes of many American citizens. Is it now going to intensify support, through increased investment, for yet another undemocratic government? In other places a demand is made that before American financial help can be given the government must become democratic. This applies to former communist regimes. It has never been suggested in the case of British rule in Ireland. On the contrary, financial and other assistance is given irrespective of whether democratic rule is conceded or not, or rather in the face of continued refusal of the British government to grant it. Where financial help is given to such a government military help is never far behind.

The continuing refusal to define violence was illustrated by the demand by Mr Ahern and others that people should not vote for Sinn Féin until the IRA ceasefire is restored. But if people refused to vote for Sinn Féin because the IRA has not called a ceasefire they would have admitted thereby that they the people do not have the right to decide freely who their elected representatives shall be. Their refusal would strengthen British determination to keep Sinn Féin out and would weaken the thrust of SDLP as well. This would make the democratic position worse, not better. The implication of such thinking is that Sinn Féin should be eliminated or weakened so as to leave the way open for an agreement between six county unionists, London and Dublin. But there is still no evidence that such an agreement could be successfully made or that it would be democratic. Weakening Sinn Féin could have the opposite result. The Fianna Fáil party in coalition with the highly conservative Progressive Democrats would probably welcome an agreement with the equally conservative unionist parties in the six counties.

The demand for better treatment of prisoners was refused by the British during the ceasefire. Its response was underlined by the repressive treatment of Roisin McAliskey. Yet another of the suggestions by the Dublin administration for showing good-will had been refused by the British. There was no sign of good-will and yet the Dublin administration kept asking and hoping for one. Confidence building gestures were absent, even the slightest of changes in the RUC suggested by Mr Ryder and Mr Cook, members of the Police Authority.

The North Report on political marching accepted the principle that in deciding whether political and religious marching should take place or not, authority did not lie with the people of any district where the marches might not be welcome but with some more remote authority appointed by government. This was another device to keep decision-making as far away from the people as possible while at the same time removing the blame for highly charged political decisions from the government.

But there comes a time when government finds it less and less easy to be absolved from blame. On Sunday 6 July 1997 the British army and the RUC by a trick carefully planned while negotiations were still going on forced an Orange march, led by clergymen, along the Garvaghy Road where residents did everything possible to prevent them. For the moment the big business and high church factions in the Orange Order had been defeated through their own timidity and the government's dishonesty. The secretary of state Mowlam, promised legislation to prevent the like occurring the following year.

People showed little sign of believing her.

For democrats in the six counties the question had now resolved itself into how and when the regime, the last surviving non-democratic statelet in the European Union, would collapse inwards through the weight of its own corruption, and how democrats could help it dissolve.

Anything less would invite another half century of government by bullying, inefficiency and greed.

# Notes

## The Setting

1   Women's Voices, *Oral History of Northern Irish Women's Health (1900–1990)*, National Union of Public Employees, Attic Press 1992, p. 81.
2   *Belfast, Belfast*, ed. Michael Hall, North Belfast History Workshop 1992, Vol. 1, p. 1
3   Interview with Mrs Wynne, West Belfast.
4   *Voices and the Sound of Drums*, Patrick Shea, Blackstaff 1983, p. 108.
5   *Guns for Ulster*, Fred H. Crawford, Foreword by Wilfred Spender, 1947. *Passim*, pp. IX–X.
6   *Paisley*, Ed Moloney and Andy Pollak, Poolbeg 1994, p. 437.

## The Imperial Bargain

1   For a detailed account of the Middle East 1919–1921 see *A Peace to End all Peace*, David Fromkin, Avon Books NY, 1989.
2   Fromkin, *op. cit.*, p. 470.
3   Fromkin, *op. cit.*, p. 17.
4   Fromkin, *op. cit.*, p. 528.
5   *Christians in Ulster*, Eric Gallagher and Stanley Worrall, Oxford University Press 1982, p. 9.
6   *International Policy Review* , Vol. 5 , No 1, Spring 1995.
7   *The Ulster Debate*, J. C. Beckett, *et al*, The Bodley Head 1972, p. 14.
8   *What Must be Done*, Robert McCartney, Athol Books 1986, p. 7.
9   *International Policy Review*, Vol 5, No 1, Spring 1995, p. 31
10  *The Truth about British Repression*, Maurice Burke, Joe McVeigh, Tomas Walsh, Des Wilson, Clergy for Justice, pp. 78.
11  The Government of Ireland Act 1920, paragraphs 2 and 3.
12  *Frongoch, the University of Revolution*, Seán O'Mahony, FDR Teoranta 1987, p. 154; Burke, *op. cit.*, p. 114.
13  *Fooled Again*, Anthony Coughlan, Mercier Press 1986, p. 33.
14  *Irish Times*, 4 January 1982.

## Myths and Mythmakers

1   *Donegal Democrat*, 11 July 1996.
2   *Christians in Ulster*, p. 15.
3   *Christians in Ulster*, p. 195.
4   Mgr Denis Faul, *Catholic Herald*, 23 August 1996.
5   *Bonfires on the Hillside*, James Kelly, Fountain Publishing 1995, p. 166.
6   *Up off their Knees*, Conn McCluskey, McCluskey and Associates 1989, p. 78.
7   *Governing Without Consensus*, Richard Rose, Faber and Faber 1971.
8   *Belfast, Portraits of a City*, Robert Johnstone, Barrie and Jenkins 1990, p. 134.
9   Johnstone, *op. cit.*, p. 49.
10  *Minority Verdict*, Maurice Hayes, Blackstaff 1995, p. 208.
11  Hayes, *op. cit.*, p. 185.

12  'Paul to the Thessalonians', 3:10–12, *Good News for Modern Man* edition.
13  Robert Johnstone, *op. cit.*, p. 125.
14  *West Belfast – The Way Forward?*, Des Wilson and Oliver Kearney, Wilson/ Kearney 1988.
15  *Church, State and Industry*, Rev. John Carson, Carson 1964.
16  Catholic Church internal documents, *passim.*

## ATTACK AND DEFENCE

1  Hayes, *op. cit.*, p. 138.
2  *Orders for the Captain?*, James Kelly, 1971, p. 111.
3  James Kelly, *op. cit.*, p. 150.
4  James Kelly, *op. cit.*, p. 11.
5  James Kelly, *op. cit.*, pp. 196, 199.

## NON-SECTARIAN MURDER

1  *Sunday Tribune*, 18 August 1996.
2  *The Dust Has Never Settled*, Robert Bryans, Honeyford Press 1992, *passim.*
3  *Spycatcher*, Peter Wright, Paul Greengrass, Heinemann Australia, 1988.

## TORTURE INTENDED

1  For an account of the Algerian war, *La Guerre d'Algerie*, Yves Courriere, Fayard, 1969, three volumes; Summary of the Algerian situation, *Political Violence*, Ed. John Darby, Nicholas Dodge, A. C. Hepburn, Appletree Press/University of Ottawa Press, 1990, chap. 13; For details of the controversy aroused by the use of torture by the French in Algeria, see for example, *Pour L'Abolition de la Torture, Action des Chretiens pour L'Abolition de la Torture, 1975*; *J'Accuse le General Massu*, Jules Roy, Editions du Seuil, 1972; *Je Denonce La Torture*, Alec Mellor, Mame, 1972; Article by Bollardiere, in *Etudes*, Mai 1972, p. 643.
2  *The Guinea Pigs*, John McGuffin, Penguin 1974, p. 133.
3  Church leaders' joint statement, 10 August 1971.
4  *Christians in Ulster*, p. 204.
5  *The Truth about British Repression*, p. 127.
6  *History of the SS*, G. S. Graber, Robert Hale, London 1996

## THE CLERICAL STATE

1  *Wylie Blue*, D. Frazer Hurst, James Clarke and Co., 1957.
2  *Guns for Ulster*, Introduction by Wilfred Spender, pp. IX, X.
3  *Wylie Blue*, p. 42.
4  Presbyterian *Confession of Faith*, first used in 1647, Ch. 25–26.
5  *Irish News*, 23 September 1995.
6  *An Episode in the History of Protestant Ulster, 1923–1947*, William Corkery, published by the author, n.d.
7  *Irish Times*, 27 April 1996
8  *The Autobiography of Terence O'Neill*, Rupert Hart-Davis, 1972, p. 67.
9  O'Neill, *op. cit.*, p. 139
10  University of Ulster Report, *Irish Times*, 9 August 1996.

11. Traditionally boycott has been recognised as a non-violent and moral instrument for communities who are otherwise relatively powerless.
12 *Christians in Ulster*, p. 41
13 *Kristallnacht, Unleashing the Holocaust,* Anthony Read and David Fisher, Papermac 1989, p. 23.
14 *Irish Man–Irish Nation,* Columban League Lectures, Mercier Press 1947, p. 18.
15 *Against the Tide,* Noel Browne, Gill and Macmillan 1986.
16 Patrick Shea, *op. cit.*, p. 162

## UNWELCOME PEACE
1 Cf. *Labour, A Party Fit for Imperialism,* Robert Clough, Counter-attack 1992, *passim.*

## AFTER THE WAR WAS OVER
1 *Those Dutch Catholics,* ed. Michael van der Plas and Henk Suer, Geoffrey Chapman 1967.
2 *Those Dutch Catholics, op. cit.,* pp. 42–43.
3 *The Church and the Irish Struggle,* Discussion with Gary Mac Eoin, Bernadette McAliskey, Des Wilson, Springhill Community House 1995, pp. 8–9.
4 *Irish News,* 9 August 1996.
5 *Irish Times,* 9 August 1996.

## STRUGGLES FOR POWER
1 Seán O'Mahony, *op. cit.*, p. 152

# No Faith in the System
## A Search for Justice
*Sr Sarah Clarke*

Paddy Hill of the Birmingham Six described Sister Sarah Clarke as *the Joan of Arc of prisoners.* This book tells her story from her childhood through the period she spent as a teacher of art in the Bower convent in Athlone and finally to her work with prisoners in British jails. Over a period of twenty-five years, Sister Sarah relentlessly pursued the cause of justice on behalf of Irish people arrested under the Prevention of Terrorism Act. In 1976 she gave up her teaching job to do full-time pastoral work with prisoners and their families. Among the thousands of prisoners with whom she worked were the Birmingham Six, the Guildford Four and the Maguire Seven. Her campaigning work frequently resulted in clashes with the Home Office and she was eventually barred from visiting prisoners but continued her work outside the prisons with wives and children of the prisoners,

This book is a testimony to the determination and courage of a woman who for many years was at odds with both the Church and State because of her perception of the appalling failings of the British criminal justice system.

# THE PATH TO FREEDOM
*MICHAEL COLLINS*

Many books have been written about the life and death of Michael Collins. *The Path to Freedom* is the only book he wrote himself.

These articles and speeches, first published in 1922, throw light not only on the War of Independence, the Civil War and the foundation of the Free State but on crucial contemporary issues.

> The actions taken indicated an over-keen desire for peace, and although terms of truce were virtually agreed upon, they were abandoned because the British leaders thought their actions indicated weakness, and they consequently decided to insist upon the surrender of our arms. The result was the continuance of the struggle.

Michael Collins on efforts to bring about a truce earlier in 1920.

# Michael Collins
## The Man Who Won the War
*T. Ryle Dwyer*

In formally proposing the adoption of the Anglo-Irish Treaty on 19 December 1921 Arthur Griffith referred to Michael Collins as 'the man who won the war', much to the annoyance of the Defence Minister Cathal Brugha, who questioned whether Collins 'had ever fired a shot at any enemy of Ireland'.

Who was this Michael Collins, and what was his real role in the War of Independence? How was it that two sincere, selfless individuals like Griffith and Brugha, could differ so strongly about him?

This is the story of a charismatic rebel who undermined British morale and inspired Irish people with exploits, both real and imaginary. He co-ordinated the sweeping Sinn Féin election victory of 1918, organised the IRA, set up the first modern intelligence network, masterminded a series of prison escapes and supervised the fundraising to finance the movement.

Collins probably never killed anybody himself, but he did order the deaths of people standing in his way, and even advocated kidnapping an American President. He was the prototype of the urban terrorist and the real architect of the Black and Tan War.